How to be Successful in Business:
A Practical Guide to Sales

How to be Successful in Business:
A Practical Guide to Sales

Adam Bradley

Dedicated to my incredible wife, Leanne, for the love and support.

About the Author

Adam Bradley is an experienced, award-winning sales director and business leader with a demonstrated history of working in the oil and gas, aerospace, defence, and industry sectors. He was born in Barnsley, South Yorkshire, and started his career in sales and marketing, after completing his teacher training back in 2006. He has since gone on to lead teams, departments and companies within the specialist materials and steel stockholding sector. He is skilled in negotiation, sales team management, engineering, supply chain management and international sales.

Adam is a strong believer in collaboration and networking to support local businesses and to promote the metals industry worldwide. He has developed a strong online presence and has been featured in many industry articles, podcasts and videos.

He is a promotor and believer in careers education and apprenticeships within manufacturing and engineering and has experience training apprentices, presenting at school assemblies, career events, teaches interview techniques and facilitates work experience. In addition to being a director at Corrosion Resistant Materials, Adam is also currently:

- Board Member of the British Stainless Steel Association
- Business Mentor and Committee Member for the Barnsley and Rotherham Chamber of Commerce
- Chairperson for the Materials Working Group – British Valve and Actuator Association
- Host of Island Networking in Rotherham

Adam has been recognized with the following awards:

- Business Growth Award – Barnsley and Rotherham Chamber of Commerce - 2019
- Queens Award for Enterprise in International Trade - 2022
- Made in Sheffield Award for Export - 2022
- Business Person of the Year - Barnsley and Rotherham Chamber of Commerce - 2022
- 50 Most Exciting Companies in Yorkshire - Insider Media - 2023
- 42 under 42 - Insider Media – 2023

Adam hopes that this book will provide a valuable resource to those in business and sales positions.

Contents

Introduction

First of all, welcome. I'm Adam and I'm here to hopefully prevent you from making some of the same mistakes I did when I first leaped into the world of business. Over the course of my career, I've accumulated a wealth of knowledge and experience that will benefit those in business, whether they're first starting out, or they've been in business for a while. I'm a huge fan of collaborative learning and believe that people from all backgrounds stand to gain a lot from the sharing of knowledge and expertise.

There's a misconception in business that you have to do it alone. I don't think that's the case at all. Running a business can be a lonely place, and through collaboration and the building of solid business relationships, the journey can be far less lonely and a whole lot simpler. There's no point reinventing the wheel and if my experience can support somebody in their business journey, then I am more than happy to do that. I've been both a mentor and a mentee, a leader and a manager, an employee and a businessman, so I know the ins and outs of the industry as well as anybody.

The aim of this book is to help you take your business to the next level. We'll cover everything you need to know in order to support your business (and yourself) to succeed. I'll share with you my successes, and my mistakes, all illustrated with real-life examples. We'll cover everything from exporting, to marketing, to business development, and everything in between. By the end of this book, you'll have a good foundation of knowledge upon which to build, and a lot of points to put into action.

Ready to dive in? Let's go.

Networking

The sharing of information or services between people, businesses, or groups.

When you mention the word 'networking' usually people fall into one of two categories. Either they LOVE networking, or they HATE it. Unfortunately, if you fall into the latter category, networking is a necessary evil. In my experience, networking is 100% essential if a business is to be successful. Whether you work in sales, or own your own business, learning how to network is a skill that will set you on the path to success.

What to Expect...

In this chapter, you will learn everything you need to know about networking. Networking is one of those things that you get better at, the more you practise, and so at the end of this chapter, you'll have the information you need to go out into the world and start networking. We will cover...

- Types of Networking
- My Top Tips
- Real-Life Examples of Networking in Action
- The Golden Rules of Networking

The Basics of Networking

We know that networking is the sharing of information or services between people, businesses or groups. But it is so much more than that. At the very core of it, networking is meeting new people, both within and outside of your industry, and getting to know one another. The main goal of networking is growth; to support professionals to grow within their careers. Current statistics suggest that around 85% of jobs are filled as a result of networking and that professionals who allocated 6 hours per week to networking said it played a crucial role in their success.

Now, you might be thinking that it would be impossible to spend six hours a week networking. There seems to be a misconception that networking isn't 'work' when, in reality, networking is one of the best uses of time for people in sales positions and small business owners. Not only does it allow you to contribute to the success of your business, but it helps you support the success of others. In other words, you reap what you sow.

The Benefits of Networking

Boiling it down to the main points, there are four key benefits of networking…

- Networking allows an exchange of ideas and knowledge.
- Networking helps you meet professionals from all backgrounds and disciplines.
- Networking can support your social well-being, particularly for solo-entrepreneurs.
- Networking can give you a considerable boost in confidence.

It's not all about making sales. In fact, that is a very small part of the equation, as you'll see in a short while. For now, let's look at the different types of networking.

Types of Networking

Networking can usually be split into two categories: online or in-person. In reality, the opportunities for networking are endless. The rise of technology means that it is easier than ever to network with professionals from all over the world, from the comfort of your own home. However, it is important that you don't overlook the opportunities for face-to-face networking as, in my opinion, there's no replacement for the deep, personal connections you can make in person. That being said, let's explore the types of networking further.

ONLINE NETWORKING

Online networking was a blessing for many people throughout the recent pandemic, myself included. While I would have preferred to steer towards in-person networking, I didn't have a choice but to focus solely on online networking. It didn't feel very natural to me at first (we're all human) but having the opportunity to network, to chat with people via video message or over the phone, and to still make connections, was of great value. It can be a considerable time saver for people in terms of commuting and it can be done on a far larger, and wider, scale, which is certainly beneficial.

There are a growing number of networking groups and websites, and don't forget social media, that you can join in order to network online. Old favourites are Facebook, LinkedIn, Twitter and Instagram. However, there are now numerous sites and companies offering online meetups and virtual networking events.

IN-PERSON NETWORKING

For me, in-person networking is where I feel the most comfortable, and the most able to make lasting connections. In-person networking is any networking that takes place face-to-face. You might be meeting an acquaintance over a coffee or attending a conference or exhibition, all of these types of events fall under this heading. Something I'm particularly passionate about are **community networking groups** aimed towards SMEs (Small or Medium Sized Enterprises) with the aim of facilitating networking and the sharing of information. Some are run privately, where you pay a small fee to attend or are charged a membership fee, while some are free. It all depends on what you're looking for and what is available in your local area. In my local area, these community networking events take on many different forms including:

1. Breakfast Networking – coffee and a bacon sandwich.

2. Curry Club – does what it says.

3. Net-walking – getting out into the wild with other like-minded business people.

4. Net-cycling – similar to walking but on bikes.

5. Having a Meal Together

The possibilities go on forever, and your local area might have some other weird and wonderful things on offer for you to participate in. The main point of the meeting is that you are making new connections, strengthening existing connections, and sharing knowledge and insight with others.

SIDE STORY: I run a small networking community group in Rotherham called Island Networking. We charge £10 per session and you get a breakfast sandwich and unlimited tea/coffee. It is very relaxed and there is plenty of opportunity for networking. There is also a couple of guest speakers so you will always learn something by attending even if you don't achieve what you set out to do from it. Networking doesn't have to be this big, scary, formal thing.

Conferences and Exhibitions are what most people think of when they hear the word 'networking'. At these events, there's often the opportunity to meet before or after the conference or exhibition is finished. As a company, Corrosion Resistant Materials has been a member of the BVAA [British Valve & Actuator Association] who run many conferences with a small desktop expo and evening meal/entertainment at night. During the day there is plenty of opportunity to chat and meet new people and businesses. This is the ideal opportunity to meet people within a similar field to your own.

Networking can take on many forms, the only criteria are that you are meeting other professionals, sharing ideas and learning from one another. I understand that networking can be quite a daunting premise if you're new to it, so I'd now like to share with you my top tips to help you put yourself out there, and feel confident when doing so.

Top Tips for Networking

1. Find the right type of networking for you.

If you hate crowds, then exhibitions and conferences might not be the best place for you to begin, for example. I've compiled a list of questions to ask yourself as you begin to figure out what type of networking would work for you, or at the very least, what you feel comfortable beginning with.

- Do you prefer face-to-face or online?
- What time of day can you, or would you like to, network?
- Do you have any particular interests or skills you'd like to develop?
- What is available to you at the present, both in-person and online?

There isn't a one size fits all approach. Don't be afraid to try a few and work out which ones are best for you.

2. Do your research and have a strategy.

Don't go into it blind. Think about what you want to achieve from networking. Do you want more business, more skills, more suppliers, more referrals, more contacts, to raise your company profile? By setting your goals and creating a strategy on how to achieve those, you'll likely have a far easier time of it. It can ensure that you are both successful, and have a decent time while doing so. Without having a plan from the start, you could be wasting your time, and nobody wants that.

Before any networking event, I always go with a set of targets of what I want to achieve. This may include who I would like to speak to, but also includes what I need help with. You will be amazed at what you can achieve in a few hours with a room full of experienced business people.

SIDE STORY: I go to many networking events and they are for different reasons.

I go to events run by the Barnsley and Rotherham Chamber of Commerce, such as the Curry Club, to share best practice, help other local businesses, and to seek new suppliers for our business. To this date, I haven't once secured any direct business from people wanting to buy metals, but I have gained lots of different things, such as suppliers for promotional goods, IT, telephones, electricians, etc. It has allowed me to raise the profile of the company by winning two Business Awards from the local chamber (Business Growth 2019 and Business Person of the Year 2022) which has given the whole company great confidence and really put us on the map. These local services are key in running a business and often go overlooked. Many people only see sales and new customers as the positive from networking.

I go to networking events held at conferences such as the ones for the BVAA. The strategy on this one is to win more business and secure more customers. The room is full of potential customers, so it is a great event to participate in for me. And, by attending, I have secured many new customers and £100,000s of business.

3. Prepare a pitch!

The importance of this cannot be overstated. Many networking events allow the opportunity to give a sixty-second, elevator pitch about you and your company. This is your time to shine, addressing the entire room and telling them who you are, what you do, and what you are looking for. Spend some time on your pitch. You only get one chance to make a first impression, right? <u>Write it down.</u> <u>Structure it. Rehearse it, over and over until it sounds natural.</u> Don't just reel off a list of features of your company, you want to draw people in, engage them, and encourage them to want to meet you after. The main outcome is that you want them to contact you later.

Instead of listing features of your company, or about yourself, you might want to tell a story, an anecdote or something special you've done this week. Basically, just set yourself apart from the crowd. You could show a video, or your product, or something visual. There are no hard and fast rules. Be creative. You want the rest of the room to sit up and listen and not just drift away. You need them to remember you after everyone else has had their sixty seconds of fame too.

4. Follow up and keep attending.

Don't just show up once, collect some phone numbers and email addresses, and never come back. That's not what networking is. Networking is about consistency; it's about showing up. The others in the group need to get to know you, so you won't have instant results. Building relationships takes time.

My advice is this: on the first day, introduce yourself to the organiser. Tell them about you, your business, and what you're looking for, and then ask them to suggest people for you to speak to. Or, better yet, ask the organiser to make the introductions. That way you can quickly get warm introductions, and referrals, and start building your network within the room.

When you're meeting with others in the group, exchange contact information and arrange to follow up with them. It is important to follow up with everybody, even if they might not be able to give you their direct business.

<u>An Example:</u>

Consider this, you meet an accountant at an event, but you already have an accountant that you're very happy with, so you might not think to follow up with them. However, this accountant might have hundreds of clients, some of whom may be good contacts for you. Think of it like the branches of a tree, or a flow chart. The more quality contacts that you make, the more deep relationships you form with others in the group, the more referrals you are likely to receive, in addition to the sharing of knowledge at these events. The more you attend the more you will be recognized and it will become easier as the weeks and months go on.

5. Collaborate and share ideas.

This is my favourite aspect of networking. So many people network to get something out of it, because they need something, which I do understand. We all need customers for a successful business. However, networking isn't only about what you can get, but it is also about what you can give. You have a unique experience, a unique set of skills and knowledge, and so you have the ability to advise, support and help other people.

Networking is the ideal opportunity for you to help others out when you can. If you help another person or business, you instantly build rapport, and they are more likely to recommend you to others or they may even hire you for a job. This way you build your network quickly, consistently and with some credibility. The best networkers I have come across are very good at this, and it is something they love to do. I'd like to think I belong in this category, but I am always learning and developing. Nobody is ever perfect.

Speak to as many people as possible, find out if you can support them in some way. Maybe you can refer them to another member of your network who is more equipped to help them, or maybe you know somebody who may be their perfect customer. In doing so, you immediately form a bond, you show that you are reliable and supportive. In other words, by supporting somebody else, you have made a fan. You have created a fan base of business people who, in essence, will be joining your sales team and creating business/referrals for you. And all because you gave something back. In the business world, there is a great phrase that would apply here. *'You have to spend to accumulate'*. Yes, this can be said about money, but it can also be applied to giving your time to others.

6. Utilise your online presence.

While it might seem like I'm a bit of a dinosaur because I prefer networking in person, I do value online networking too, especially since the lockdowns. Being active online, particularly on social media, can support your networking mission. An example of this might be, telling your online network that you're attending (or running) an event in a few days. People may attend because they want to catch up with you, or because they weren't aware the event was taking place prior to your post. Sharing updates after an event is equally as important: share photos, stories, information about the event. Tag your new contacts too. This can help to form relationships prior to you reaching out and following up with them. In doing so, organisers of the event will be thankful too, especially if it brings attention to their events.

A Quick Note on the Power of Sharing

Networking isn't just about making connections, it's about sharing knowledge and skills with your peers. Despite having years of industry experience, I still come away from networking events having learned something new. When you go in with an open mind, forgoing any ego you have, and are ready to learn, you'll come away with so much more than new connections. The same goes for sharing what you know. We all have something to share, no matter how new we are to the game. Our unique insights and experiences make each and every person in a networking space a valuable person to know. I understand that going into networking events can feel a little intimidating, especially if you're fairly new to business. However, I promise you that you have something valuable to offer, and also you'll come away with a hell of a lot of useful information and contacts, if you open yourself up to that.

The Golden Rules of Networking

If you follow these golden rules, you won't go far wrong. It might be useful to read them just before you go into a networking event to keep them fresh in your mind. There's nothing complicated here, but in my experience, these points are where people can sometimes go wrong.

1. Show up early. It gives you more chance to talk to people as they arrive.

2. Don't try to make a sale. Remember, the aim is to get contacts and follow up.

3. Don't jump into other conversations, it's just rude.

4. Stand when presenting, especially on your sixty-second pitch.

5. Remember to smile!

6. Listen to others and be interested in what they're saying, don't just talk about yourself.

7. Ask questions to put others at ease. For example, what brings you to the event today?

8. Take business cards and make them easy to get to. Don't leave them in a bag or car!

TOP TIP: *When you receive a business card, ask for two and explain that it is so you can pass their details onto someone else if needed. This instantly builds a good collaborative relationship.*

9. In a free networking environment, stand in an open area away from the bar, eating area or door. You will find more people will come and chat to you if you are accessible.

10. First impressions count. Consider the dress code for the event, offer handshakes, be calm and upbeat/positive.

Words of Wisdom from People Wiser than Me!

We'll end each chapter with quotes that will benefit you moving forward. I'm a huge fan of not reinventing the wheel and so if there are learning opportunities to be had from the words of people far wiser than me, why not make the most of that? Here are some quotes that I like to keep at the forefront of my mind when networking.

"The currency of real networking is not greed but generosity."

Keith Ferrazzi

"Networking is not about just connecting people. It's about connecting people with people, people with ideas, and people with opportunities."

Michele Jennae

"My Golden Rule of Networking is simple: Don't keep score."

Harvey Mackay

"Networking is an enrichment program, not an entitlement program."

Susan RoAne

Summary

Networking is the sharing of information or services between people, businesses, or groups. It is so much more than making contacts or sales, it is about forming relationships, sharing your knowledge and experiences, and learning from others. Networking is one of those things where you get out of it what you put into it. If you go to one networking event with some phone numbers and never bother going back, you're not going to get the true benefit of it. My advice would be to throw yourself into networking, put aside some time every week to focus solely on networking – both on supporting others, and forming connections. Networking is my favourite part of my job because it's such a powerful experience.

Three takeaways...
1. **Networking is give and take, not just take.**
2. **Be prepared!**
3. **Find what works for you.**

Customer Visits

Visiting with a contact, buyer, or company in order to engage directly with them and build a positive working relationship with them.

Customer visits have taken a back burner in today's modern post-Covid world. Many companies have migrated online to conduct meetings with their customers. Platforms such as Zoom and Microsoft Teams have become the norm for having face-to-face meetings with the customer, with many companies forgoing in-person customer visits altogether. While I understand that online meetings are far easier – they can be done from the comfort of your office, there's less travel time, and in some cases, you don't have to fly halfway across the world – I do believe that in-person visits are an incredibly important aspect of most businesses. That's not to say that online meetings aren't important too. There's a time and place for them, and they're a great thing to have in your sales toolbox. But they're no replacement for in-person meetings.

What to Expect...

Learning how to organise, structure and conduct customer visits is something that will benefit anybody within a sales or management position within their company. In this chapter, we will cover...

- The Benefits of Customer Visits
- My Top Tips
- Real-Life Examples
- The Aftermath of Customer Visits

A Bit of Background Information

Customer visits are a considerable aspect of my role as a director of my company. While I now believe that I have customer visits down to an art form, it wasn't always this way. As with anything in life, understanding how to conduct customer visits is a learning curve. In sharing my experiences, including my mistakes, I will support you to skip a few steps ahead of me when I first got started about fifteen years ago. Back then, customer visits were the norm and as a sales representative for a company, you would be expected to visit your customers once or twice a year, independent of where they were based. A sales representative's sole purpose was to visit with them, engage with them, and ultimately sell to them. When I first started, I shadowed more experienced sales reps to learn how to do the job. As you do when you're first starting out, I believed their example to be exactly what to do. In hindsight, this wasn't the case. So, on my first customer visits, in Scotland, this is what I did...

1. Email to book an appointment.

2. Once booked, I'd write the appointment in my calendar. I'd try to fit another four or five appointments in that day too, to make the most of time. I'd also have a few in reserve, where I could just pop by if I had a gap in time.

3. On the day of the visit, I would dress in my suit and tie, pack brochures, business cards, and make sure I had my trusty notebook and pen.

4. On arriving at the customer's site I would give the customer a PowerPoint presentation, brochure, and business card, and advise them to send enquiries.

5. I would then leave and wait until the customer sent their enquiries. If they did, then I'd declare victory.

This sounds like fairly standard practice, right? And it did work, on rare occasions. I think this image still puts customers off from allowing sales reps on site. I can't blame them, really. This approach is outdated, time-consuming, and rarely has a positive outcome for either party. Don't worry, over the years I have adapted my approach to customer visits. I've learned from my mistakes and in doing so, I've secured new customers and hundreds of thousands of pounds in business as a direct result of conducting customer visits, and conducting them well.

The Basics of Customer Visits

Customer visits don't have to be super complicated. Later in the chapter, I'll give you a foolproof step-by-step guide on how to conduct your customer service visits. For now, let's look at the benefits of customer visits and why I think they should be a part of your sales structure.

1. **An opportunity to better understand the customer.**

If you're looking at customer visits in terms of making immediate sales, then you're looking at them from the wrong angle. Customer visits are the perfect opportunity to engage directly with your contact, buyer or company. The visit is your chance to obtain as much information about them as you can. Think of it as a fact-finding mission. Ask about their business, of course, but also ask about them as people and take a genuine interest. What you learn from this meeting will not only be useful to you later, but it will help you to build rapport. There are three important things you must find out…

I. What does the company do?

II. What issues are the company currently facing?

III. What plans do the company have for the future?

Alongside this information, get to know your contact – their family, their hobbies, their holidays, and all that other fun stuff. This is critical if you are going to build a good relationship with them. One of the most important things anybody ever said to me is this… ***People buy from people.*** Yes, there are other factors to consider in making a sale, but at the end of the day we are all human beings and we are far more likely to buy from people we like and who we consider friends.

2. The chance to demonstrate that you, and your company, are experts in your field.

Now, this doesn't necessarily mean giving a PowerPoint presentation about your company and all the ways in which you are the best. I don't want to demonise PowerPoints, they are handy sometimes, but a customer visit is not the time for them, in my experience. In a customer meeting, you should be demonstrating your value. The first step is listening to your customer and responding when you feel you can add something and help them. The whole reason for sales interactions is to help your customer solve issues that they are currently facing. If you solve their problems, they will buy from you, without you having to *sell* them anything. So, listen and offer solutions.

<u>An Example (or two):</u>

- One thing I always ask when visiting manufacturing companies is, 'Are there any grades of materials you are struggling to find at the moment?' This is specific to my industry, I'm aware, but bear with me. If the customer says, 'Yes - Alloy 800', for example, I know that I can then step in and offer solutions. I can, through good product knowledge, impress the customer by knowing about the material and where best to source it.

- Another approach is to offer solutions to problems they have that fall outside of your company's remit. For example, I sell metal but I have a large network that I can fall back on. My customer might say, 'Our IT system isn't great at the moment,' or, 'the forklift keeps breaking down'. If you can help with these issues, and recommend someone to them who can solve their issue, you will build that trust. It is then more likely that when they need your services, they will remember you and send you that enquiry.

3. Motivation for you and your business.

A customer visit can give you a great sense of achievement and energy. Interacting with customers and learning from them can give you a huge boost. So often I come back from visiting customers and I have a whole heap of new ideas that I want to implement. By visiting customers, I have seen new working practices, new systems, new machines, shopfloor layouts etc. It gives you a chance to see how other businesses perform and do things, and it can recharge your batteries and reignite your passion. You will often see first-hand how your customers actually use your product. In my field of metals sales, I get to see parts for planes, motorcars, submarines etc, and get a real sense of fulfilment that my 'lump of metal' has been turned into a beautiful part which in turn may end up on an aeroplane or spaceship. It brings excitement and a real-life experience that is hard to get from just phone or Teams calls.

4. Gain knowledge about your competition.

I would wager that your customer doesn't only buy from you. They likely buy from your competition too. In my sector, no single manufacturing company can buy all of their steel from just one company. There are many reasons for this, but mostly it is down to cash flow, credit limits and stock availability. Of course, you want to see a good percentage of the work, and understand what you need to do in order to secure this, but it can also be helpful to know what (and why) your customers are buying from your competitors. Perhaps a competitor quotes quicker, they package better, they update on a more regular basis. Whatever the reason is, finding out these tidbits of information can help you improve your business and what you offer. Nobody is perfect and feedback such as this is invaluable.

Your contact may not wish to share information about your competitors, which is fair enough. However, there are ways to gather this information in a slightly different way. By asking open questions, such as 'What is your ideal turnaround?', for example, they may say that your competitor has a turnaround time of thirty minutes, but as long as they have the product on the same day, they are happy. You were therefore able to gain some information that supports you moving forward.

The benefits of customer visits extend out into all aspects of your business, from implementing feedback, to gaining knowledge about competitors, to forming mutually beneficial relationships with the customer. It is not all about immediate sales, but about the byproduct of the customer visit. Hopefully, this has been enough to convince you that face-to-face customer visits are not a thing of the past. Maybe you're even feeling revved up and want to get on with them. But you should slow down, let me share with you how to make your customer visits successful. Don't just run in there all guns blazing, take some time to learn how to plan, conduct and follow up your customer visits. Give yourself the best chance of success.

How to Have Successful Customer Visits

We'll split this into three sections: The Run-Up, The Day-Of and The Aftermath. If you follow my suggestions here, you'll not be able to go too far off course.

THE RUN-UP

Benjamin Franklin once said, *'By failing to prepare, you are preparing to fail.'* What you do in the run-up to customer visits, is almost as important as what you do during the visit itself. In preparing, you are giving yourself a headstart, ensuring you get off on the right foot with the customer. It's a simple process that everybody who is doing customer visits should be doing.

1. Identify who you want to visit and why.

You may want to visit your top ten customers, or companies, in your pipeline. Alternatively, you might have met somebody at a networking event or exhibition and feel that it would be good to visit them and learn more about them. Essentially, you should have a reason for wanting to visit with a customer, it shouldn't be a case of, 'Oh, I should probably visit so-and-so.' This is essential, as if you don't have a focus for your visit, how can it be successful? Gone are the days when you can just stop in at a business, have a cup of tea, and try to sell them something. Maybe you know they have visited your website, or seen your LinkedIn post, or met you at a conference. If this is the case, then they will already have some knowledge of you, and a customer visit is a logical step.

TOP TIP: *Visit companies that are already trading with you or companies that you have already interacted with in some capacity. There is a greater chance of them choosing to do business with you, if this is the case. I wasted a lot of time in my younger years by visiting companies that weren't the right fit – they hadn't heard of me, and I knew nothing about them. Don't waste your time, learn from my mistakes.*

2. Set up the meeting.

Once you have your list of companies that you want to visit, you have to organise an appointment that suits both of you. This might sound simple, but there's an art to it. The best way to do this is to organise the meeting via phone, unless your contact prefers email communication (and some do). First of all, you ask them if they'd be open to a visit and then you ask if there is a convenient time/date for them. This will give you a fixed date in your diary. You're probably thinking, *but I want to visit four or five customers on one day so that I can make the most out of it.* This is good practice, and is something I've always done. However, I always start by asking when would be convenient for the customer/contact as the meeting is more likely to be a success if the meeting is convenient for them. If you already have a meeting booked in at the date/time they suggest, you can be honest with them and offer an alternative – this is why it is easier over the phone, rather than by email. By giving them control over the meeting first, you build trust and rapport, and as they organised the date/time, they are less likely to cancel at the last minute. During this stage, decide who will be present in the meeting. Maybe somebody from the technical side of the company or somebody from accounts would be a great addition, for example.

TOP TIP*: Make sure to send your customer an Outlook meeting request so that it appears in both of your diaries.*

3. Prepare for the meeting.

This is the most important part of the process. You need to gather as much information as possible about the company. This may include their order book, previous orders, complaints, enquiries, etc. You need to come across as knowledgeable about their interaction with your company, so do your research. If they are new to you, then do all you can to research the company. Use their website, their social media, to find out what the company is currently doing.

Maybe they've launched a new project, taken on more staff, have won an award. Going into a customer visit armed with this information will help you predict, as much as possible, what will be discussed during the meeting. It also shows that you care about your customers. You can never be over-prepared, but you can be under-prepared. Treat it like you would if you were doing an interview – what would you like to know about the company before you interviewed with them? If you are to deliver a presentation (this is still needed in some circumstances) then make sure you have it well-rehearsed, backed up and also printed out.... just in case your IT fails. Plan for all eventualities.

4. Some final preparations…

Here are some final things to consider in the run-up to your customer visit.

- Check where the meeting will take place and ensure you have an accurate address. Do this directly with your contact, and don't rely on their website address.

SIDE STORY: Here's an opportunity for you to learn from my mistakes. Over the years, I've booked a few meetings and turned up at the site, only to learn that the company is no longer based at that site, even if their website (and orders!) says they still are.

I once tried to visit a customer in the Czech Republic at their site near Prague. I checked the website and got the address and plummed this into the SAT NAV. On arriving at the factory, I was greeted with locked gates and no one on site. On ringing the customer, I found out they had moved four months ago and forgot to update their website. Their new site was an hour away in the other direction. This made me late to the meeting and all the other meetings that day. A total disaster and all because I didn't check where I was meeting with the customer.

- Plan an agenda – It is always good practice to have an agenda for what you'd like to discuss in the meeting. If this is an existing customer, then you may have some things to address with them anyway. If you haven't worked with them yet, this is a great chance to create some rapport.

- Plan your outfit and dress to impress. Now, I wouldn't wear a shirt and tie unless I thought this was what the client was expecting. Dress for your audience, and your location. For example, if you were meeting on a worksite you might wear work boots, your company jacket and a high-vis. However, if you were meeting in a boardroom, you might wear a shirt and tie. It is better to be over-dressed than under-dressed.

- Pack well and be prepared. Business cards, brochures, and anything else you'll need (for example, printouts of your PowerPoint, if you're doing one). There is nothing worse than getting into a meeting and your customer presents you with a business card only for you to have forgotten yours.

THE DAY-OF

So you have prepared well, you have booked that meeting, and you are dressed to impress. You are nervous but want to arrive calm and make the visit a success. Here are my top tips for what to do during that all-important customer visit...

1. **Be on time.** This is SO IMPORTANT. If you're late, it gives a bad first impression and first impressions count. On a similar note, don't show up super early either because it can be an inconvenience to your contact. I aim to arrive 10-15 minutes early, in case of traffic or if I get lost. That way I have plenty of time to get my things together and find the reception.

2. **Be courteous with everybody you come across.** Be polite and get to know the person on the reception. Ask them how they are, how their day has been etc. This goes a long way in giving your company a good image from the off.

3. **Don't sell or pitch.** Allow the conversation to flow naturally. Don't force anything. Back in the day I would sit down with the customer and start my pitch. Don't do that! Learn about the company, the person, and try to leave with as much information about them (and their needs) as possible.

4. **Listen more than speak.** In your meeting you want your contact to do the majority of speaking. Do not jump in when you see an opportunity to tell your story. Absorb everything and add value. If what you are saying doesn't add value, solve an issue or build rapport, then leave it out. By listening to what your customer says you can learn a great deal about them and their business.

5. **Upsell and cross-sell.** Yes, I know this contradicts what I said a second ago. But I don't mean upsell then and there. Your customer might mention an issue that you weren't aware of, an issue that your company

could offer a solution for. This is an opportunity to mention that you have a solution they may wish to explore.

An Example:

In my particular field, cross-selling would be to sell them different grades of materials, ones you are not currently selling them. Maybe you didn't know they needed them or your customer didn't know you sold them. Whereas, upselling would be to sell value-added services such as boring, turning, and testing. To be able to do this it is important to know what they are doing with your product (in my case steel) when they buy it. If my customer tells me when they receive the material they send it for heat treatment, this is my chance to say 'we can do this for you' and help them further.

6. **Leave on a positive note and agree on the next steps.** This is really important so you have something to follow up with after your visit. At this stage, you might also ask about referrals. Don't be afraid to ask for referrals. If you have a happy customer, they may well tell you of another company that might want your service or product. If you don't ask you don't get. It's all about how you leave your customer, or contact, feeling after the visit. Ensuring you leave on a positive note, thanking them for their time and saying it was lovely to meet them, as well as creating a plan of action moving forward, gives a great impression of you and your company.

THE AFTERMATH

It can be easy to forget the aftermath of a meeting. If you're still relatively new to customer visits, you might just feel relieved that it is over with. However, what you do in the aftermath is essential in continuing a positive relationship with that contact or company.

TOP TIP: *Straight after the meeting, allow yourself some time to make notes and record the details of what was said. Make clear and actionable points that you can deal with when you return to the office. If you don't do this, you may mix up meetings or forget to implement something you promised the customer.*

After the meeting, you should...

- Follow up with them on the same day, or the next day. Thank your contact for seeing you via email or phone. This is another touch point and a chance to build rapport. During this email, or phone call, outline the actions you discussed and what you will be doing about them. Give a timeframe and make sure these points are actioned.

- Keep in regular contact with them. You have now built a relationship with your customer, so make the most of it. Don't let all that hard work go to waste. Ring them, or email, every few weeks for a chat and to see if you can help them. In doing so, it is more likely that they will remember you, trust you further, and send those enquiries and orders to you.

Words of Wisdom from People Wiser than Me!

Sometimes, we all need to take a step back and let people who are wiser than we are take the lead. So, I'm going to do that now. Here are my top three quotes about sales. I remind myself of these often. It can help me go into customer visits with the right perspective and in the right frame of mind.

'We don't want to push our ideas on to customers, we simply want to make what they want.'
Laura Ashley

'I've learned that people will forget what you said, people will forget what you did, but people will never forget how you made them feel.'
Maya Angelou

'Happy customers are your biggest advocates and can become your most successful sales team.'
Lisa Masiello

Summary

Customer visits are the perfect opportunity to <u>visit with a contact, buyer or company in order to engage directly with them and build a positive working relationship with them.</u> Building a successful company is all about creating great relationships with customers and contacts. Customer visits are the ideal way to communicate that you are competent, knowledgeable, and a good person to work with. By preparing well, and avoiding the pitfalls I fell straight into when I first started, you are setting yourself up for success. Go into the customer visits with the aim of understanding your customer better and forming a good relationship. The sales will happen organically, if you are able to portray yourself, and therefore your business, in a good light.

Three takeaways...
1. **People buy from people.**
2. **Listen more than you speak.**
3. **Be prepared.**

Exhibitions

A gathering of businesses, professionals and representatives with the view to showcase goods, and exchange knowledge, products and services.

Exhibitions (sometimes referred to as 'trade shows') have been crucial sales and marketing tools for centuries. They were popularised back in medieval Europe as a method for exchanging commodities. While they are run very differently now, the similarities between modern and historical exhibitions can still be seen. Think of the phrase 'if it ain't broke, don't fix it'. However, there are certain ways in which you can get the most out of exhibitions. In this chapter, I will share with you exactly what to do, and what not to do. Many industries have their own exhibitions. They are a great way to catch up with existing contacts, as well as to make more contacts. You already know my views on networking, and exhibitions are a great way to practise what you learned in the networking chapter of this book. Through exhibitions, you can secure new business, as well as new suppliers, all under one roof. You are able to reach out to many businesses in a very short time without having to take the time to visit each and every one of them. Exhibitions should be key in both your travel plans and also marketing plans.

What to Expect...

Exhibitions are a world of their own. Learning how to navigate them, in order to make the most of your time and energy, will ensure that you gain the most from attending and/or exhibiting. In this chapter, we will cover...

- The Top Five Reasons Exhibitions are Essential
- Top Tips for Attending Exhibitions
- Top Tips for Exhibiting
- What to do After Exhibitions

Why Are Exhibitions Important?

Now, I would argue that exhibitions aren't just important, they are essential. There are five key reasons why you should be attending exhibitions – both to exhibit and to visit.

1. Generating sales and leads.
2. Building rapport with potential customers and suppliers.
3. Networking opportunities.
4. Building brand awareness.
5. Gaining further industry knowledge – this is particularly great for new or less-experienced members of your team.

And, if I'm being honest with you, attending an exhibition is usually just a great experience. It's a really good way of getting you motivated and fired up. Surrounding yourself with people from the same, or similar, industries really does have many benefits, in addition to those key ones listed above. They tend to be really positive for all the people involved, and are an ideal opportunity for team-building and bonding, and also for learning more about your competition.

Top Tips for Visiting Exhibitions

There are hundreds, if not thousands, of exhibitions every year. And, of course, they take place all around the globe. They might be called slightly different names, trade fairs, expos, trade shows, but they all come under the same bracket. They are the opportunity for businesses to show their products/services, to network, to learn and develop, to meet suppliers and buyers and to generate leads. Some are small, some are incredibly large, some are free and some charge, some are for a day and others for a whole week. There are many different options out there, and finding the right exhibition/s for you is the key to your success. If you're attending an exhibition as a visitor, which means that you're not going to present or run a stall, then these are my top tips for you…

BEFORE

1. Do your research.

This is twofold, first you have to narrow down a list of exhibitions you wish to visit. Research the exhibitions available to your industry. Which ones do your customers/suppliers/competitors exhibit at? This will give you a good measure of which ones are worth attending.

Once you have narrowed down which exhibitions you want to visit, then you need to research the event. Don't just show up without any plan in place. By planning ahead, as much as possible, you will make the most of your time when you are there. Most exhibitions will publish a list of exhibitors prior to the event, you will therefore be able to see which companies have stands and who will be giving talks/speeches. You can then plan your route around the event accordingly.

TOP TIP: *Plan around ten minutes per stand. In an eight-hour day, that means you can generally hit around 48 exhibitors. If it is a larger event, I will give myself two days. The plan will be rough and you may have to make amendments on the day, but having it ahead of time will make the day run far smoother for you.*

2.   Make some appointments with exhibitors.

This is a great way to build some rapport before you even attend the event. I would do this for my top ten targets, for example. This gives you a chance to promote your company before you attend, on the day the conversation will be easier because you are already familiar to them. It also enables you to have a clear goal of what you want to achieve by visiting the exhibition. With exhibitions, it is near impossible to book a specific time slot because both of you will be busy. However, I tend to say that I will visit with them on a specific day, or in the AM/PM. This can help to avoid missing the exhibitors that are your priorities, as often people won't be there for the whole event, etc.

Remember, also, to allow yourself leeway with the timings. Don't plan things down to the last minute or second because things will always come up that you didn't anticipate. Maybe you bump into a contact you didn't expect to see there, or you find yourself in a really interesting conversation with an exhibitor that you didn't anticipate having anything in common with. If you can, check out who is visiting too. A lot of exhibitions will have Facebook or LinkedIn events and you can check out who is attending as a visitor, not just an exhibitor, as they may well be your current or potential customers or suppliers. I have been to many a trade show where I have secured more business from those visiting than those exhibiting. See it as a good networking opportunity across all levels.

3. Shout about it on social media.

Before you attend an event, tell the whole world you're attending. If you do this, people are more likely to recognise you and may want to reach out and speak with you. Many exhibitions will have their own social media pages and a hashtag. Follow the pages and the hashtags, it will give you additional insight into the day. By shouting about the event on social media, you may also become recognisable to the event's organisers, and this is always of great benefit.

THE DAY OF

1. Dress the part.

This is so simple, yet so effective. Wear branded clothes, this way you raise brand awareness simply by being there. People may not recognise you, but they will recognise the company. I believe that wearing branded clothing helps you to look professional too. A final piece of advice on this… wear comfy shoes! You'll be on your feet most of the day, more than likely.

2. Arrive early.

Trade shows are often slow to get started, have a crazy middle and then tail off towards the end. The best time to speak to exhibitors will be when they are at their quietest as they are more likely to want to chat with you. This is when the best interactions take place, and the best relationships are formed. Do yourself a favour and get there early, it will be well worth the early start.

3. Don't approach a busy stand.

This is where you need to be flexible with the plan you made previously. By approaching a busy stand, you are less likely to be able to have a decent conversation with the exhibitors. The chances are that you will not be well-received and you might not get to speak to the right person. First impressions do count. Circle back to them at a time when they are quieter.

4. Wait for somebody at your target stand to approach you.

I understand that it can be quite intimidating walking up to a stand and trying to start a conversation. Usually, somebody will approach you and ask if they can help you. This is the ideal time to introduce yourself and start a conversation.

5. Don't sell.

This is a big one! Remember, the companies you are visiting are exhibiting. They are, therefore, looking to make sales themselves. They may not want to speak to suppliers. Use the time as an opportunity to find out more about the company and what they do. More often than not, the stand will be full of salespeople. And, if I know one thing about salespeople, it is that they love to talk about what they do. By doing this you may find a new opportunity and be able to move the conversation onto what you do. However, this is not the objective. See it as an opportunity to gather information.

6. Use social media.

As you did before you attended, use social media to communicate that you're there. Check yourself into the event. Post a photo. This is good publicity for both yourself and for the event. You may even find that people reach out to you – other visitors and exhibitors.

TOP TIP: *Comment on exhibitors' posts. Every single exhibitor there will put something on LinkedIn, for example. If you comment and like the post, it will build good rapport and will open up the lead straight away.*

7. Be memorable.

You can do this in many different ways. In the past, I have given out some giveaways, postcard brochures, or even worn something that stands out. Remember, the most important thing when reaching out to new people is to be remembered. If you do this, you are more likely to be contacted after. It is at this point that you can continue the sales journey.

AFTERMATH

The fun doesn't stop just because the exhibition does. This is a really important stage and is so often overlooked. You have met loads of people, gathered information and have a pocket full of business cards. So what do you do now? Within a few days of the exhibition make sure you follow up with each of your new contacts. A quick phone call or email to touch base can go a long way. Make sure you make the follow-up personal in some way and PLEASE DO NOT JUST SEND A BROCHURE. You might want to mention something you chatted about or what you enjoyed about meeting them. Steer clear of anything generic as it just doesn't work. This follow-up process is a significant aspect of the sales journey and keeping the conversation going is imperative. Be proactive. If you wait to be contacted, you may never hear from them again. This is your chance to make the hard work pay off and to make sure your visit was successful.

Top Tips for Exhibiting at Exhibitions

If you're choosing to exhibit at an exhibition, planning and execution are key. A lot of thought needs to go into how you present your company, as well as ensuring that you attend the right sort of exhibitions.

SIDE STORY: Over the years, I have attended and exhibited at too many exhibitions to count. Some were small desktop ones where you take along a few pop-ups, a table and some giveaways. Whereas others have been huge exhibitions. I started small, with the desktop ones. This was the logical first step. They might have around twenty to thirty exhibitors and a couple of hundred visitors. At Corrosion Resistant Materials, initially, as a small company, the outlay for the event was small and the return on this investment was quick. The overall cost for the stand, space, travel, etc, was low and it didn't take long to make the money back, and then some.

We then moved to larger exhibitions. With larger exhibitions, such as international trade fairs, the costs are often considerably higher. There tends to be 300-400 exhibitors and thousands of visitors. The first large exhibition I planned at Corrosion Resistant Materials was CHEMUK in 2022 at the NEC. The reason for this was that there were around 50 of our customers exhibiting there, lots of our targets were exhibiting, and also some of our competitors. The total cost of everything to exhibit was around £10,000 but we secured five new customers and sales in excess of £50,000 so it more than paid for itself. It also gave us a better platform moving forward and made others sit up and see that we were growing.

Whether you're choosing to exhibit in a small or large exhibition, here are my top tips for you. I'm sure you can already guess what the first one is…

1. Do your research and find the right exhibition for you.

There are hundreds of different exhibitions out there. Choosing the wrong exhibition can be a very costly mistake. My advice would be to go and visit a few throughout the year and then if one stands out to you, look to exhibit at that one next year. If you have been to it previously you will see the types of companies who attend and so you'd know whether you would fit in. Also, from my experience, if you get something from it from visiting, you will get more from exhibiting.

2. Book the right spot.

Finding and booking the right space in the hall is crucial, and it is something not many people consider. I always recommend a corner space because people will walk past you in both directions and your stand will be open, which stops visitors from feeling pinned in and claustrophobic. I have exhibited in both middle and corner stands and I've found that corner stands are by far superior, so if you can bag one, do. They can be more expensive, but they are worth it.

TOP TIP: *Consider the layout of the hall. Will your stand be near an area where people network? Will it be near the coffee shop or the entrance/exit? By choosing a stall near an area where people congregate, you will have a better chance of people visiting you and finding you.*

3. Make sure your brand stands out.

The main thing is that you want your message to be clear. Don't leave room for any confusion about who you are or what you do. I tend to prefer stand designs that have more pictures/graphics than words. You want people to clearly know what you do and what you can offer to them. Maybe even consider having a TV (or more than one) with videos playing, as this will help you to share your story more clearly.

The stands that do the best and stand out the most are the ones with an interactive element of some kind. Maybe a spin-the-wheel game, a speaker presentation or even barista coffee. There are so many options out there to make your brand stand out. I've even seen companies dress up their employees in costumes and have them hand out brochures. It might sound like a gimmick (because it is) but it works.

When designing your stand, less is more. It is better to have a big open space where people can come and chat. Too much on your stand and it will feel cramped and people will just walk straight past. Have a few examples of what your company does but keep them more for talking points and don't try to put everything you sell on there.

4. Take a large team.

As a general rule of thumb, if you have a 3x3m stand then you'd probably benefit from 4 or 5 people. This means that you can have people at the stand and also people around the hall speaking to other exhibitors. You should all be wearing branded clothing. At least one person should always be at the stand. Never leave it unattended. Also, somebody should always be walking through the hall. People see them in branded clothing and think, 'I'll pop to their stand.' It's all about networking and this helps you to stand apart from the crowd.

5. Choose the right marketing material.

Brochures and business cards are a given, but don't forget giveaways. People love free pens and other nicknacks. It helps to get your name out there and will jog people's memories when they return home or back to their office. A good giveaway will always drive people to your stand and again will help people remember who you are in the future.

6. Promote your attendance.

I've said it before, and I'll say it again. Promote on your social media that you'll be attending. Tell the world that you're doing it, which stand you'll be on and who out of your team will be there. And also remember to post throughout the day too. This helps you to get a steady flow of people throughout the day. It also promotes the event and will make the organisers happy. You could approach the event organisers about being a part of their advertisements or even about having a speaker slot. Most exhibitions have a conference attached to them and speaking at these can be a perfect way to promote your business.

After the Exhibition

By this point, you know what I'm going to say. The aftermath is just as important as the event itself. Follow up. Don't be complacent. Make your hard work pay off for you. By keeping the conversation open, you are keeping yourself on their radar which will repay you in dividends in the future, if not immediately.

Words of Wisdom from People Wiser than Me!

It's important to learn from the experts. And, while I do like to think I'm an expert in this field (I certainly have a lot of experience), there are people who have said some really wise words that would be pertinent here. Allow me to share them with you.

'People do not buy goods and services. They buy relations, stories and magic.'
Seth Godin

'Don't design what you like, design for your audience and what will best engage and communicate with them.'
Marlys Arnold

'Be audacious and memorable. But smart...and relevant.'
Ken Krogue

Your booth is intended to be a backdrop, not a brochure. This can't be overstated; people walking by should be able to instantly recognize who you are and what you do. It's your booth staff's job to take it from there.'
Tim Asimos

Summary

An exhibition is a <u>gathering of businesses, professionals and representatives with the view to showcase goods, and exchange knowledge, products and services.</u> It is, therefore, the perfect opportunity to expand your business, to network and to learn. Don't just throw yourself into the next exhibition you spot. Do your research and find out which ones will be the best use of your time. Which ones are your customers/competitors/suppliers attending? Start by visiting exhibitions, this will help you to learn which ones are worth exhibiting at the next year. Make the most of the experience and be open to learning from it.

Three takeaways…
1. **Do your research and be prepared.**
2. **Social media is your friend!**
3. **Make your brand stand out.**

Marketing

The activity of promoting and selling products or services, including market research and advertising. The act of attracting potential customers to a product or service.

Marketing is a key aspect of any business. It boils down to making sure that potential customers know about the products and services that you have on offer to them. But it is more than that, it's about creating the desired image for your company. First impressions count, and marketing is one of the ways in which people will first come across your company. It is therefore imperative to get your marketing right.

What to Expect...

There are many different facets to marketing. Understanding how to make marketing work for you, in the context of your business and your goals, will help you to implement marketing in a way that supports the development of your company. In this chapter, we will cover...

- What Marketing Is
- The Different Types of Marketing
- The Importance of Marketing
- My Top Ten Marketing Tips

What is Marketing?

Let's go back to basics. When you hear the word 'marketing' people have different assumptions and definitions about what it is, and what is included under this umbrella term. Marketing can take on many different forms. Using a single type of marketing in isolation will rarely get the results you hope for. In order to bring the most traffic to your company, using different marketing strategies in conjunction, and ensuring you are covering all your bases (for lack of a better term) makes your company as visible as it possibly can be. Marketing refers to **all of the activities** you undertake to promote the buying/selling of a product/service.

Types of Marketing

Content Marketing –

This is where a company creates written content, usually for their website. It may take the form of blog posts, for example. The content will focus on answering a particular question or solving a problem a customer may have. In my line of work, this may be something such as a potential customer wanting to know what heat treatment is. They search the web with their question and your content comes up as a valuable resource. The simple fact is that you helped them when they had a question and therefore when they enter the 'buy' phase, they will return to your company. It's a great way to build trust and open the door to new clients. It is also a great way to get your name out there amongst potential customers who may have an interest in your particular area of business. If they see you as a trusted and valid resource, they'll remember that.

Social Media Marketing –

You guessed it, this is marketing done on social media. There are so many different social media platforms out there, LinkedIn, Facebook, Instagram, Twitter, TikTok, and many more than I'm sure I'm forgetting. All companies, no matter how small, should have a social media presence. Social media is free (unless you choose to pay for ads), making it an invaluable resource. The key with social media is to be present and regular. Posting sporadically won't have the same impact as posting on a regular basis. This supports you to build a strong following, and increases your chances of getting your business in front of potential customers. The tool that I use the most is LinkedIn. I'll cover LinkedIn in more depth in a later chapter, but for now, know that (as part of a further social media presence) it can support you in creating a positive image of your company.

Search Engine Optimisation –

These three letters – SEO – you'll see knocking around a lot nowadays. SEO is the process of making your website do the hard work for you. It becomes another salesperson and attracts potential new customers to your company. The definition of SEO is, '*the process of maximizing the number of visitors to a particular website by ensuring that the site appears high on the list of results returned by a search engine.*' This is done through the process of the inclusion of keywords within the content on your website. It can be quite a tricky thing to get a hang of, and it isn't just a case of writing 'corrosion resistant materials' as many times as possible on your website, unfortunately. You can pay experts to support you with this, if you're not the most computer literate person. Essentially, the most important thing is to include your keywords throughout your website as much as possible, while still making sure it sounds organic. In order to do this, think about what it is that you offer. What would your potential customers be Googling? These are the keywords and phrases you want to include on your website. A great way to do this is through blog posts and frequently asked questions.

SIDE STORY: I have recently upgraded our website and SEO was a huge part of the build. I put several FAQ sections on it and put as many questions (and answers) as possible so that when a potential customer has a particular question, the search engine may show our website near the top of Google. How many people do this day to day? They have a problem and turn to Google to answer it. They may have a look at the first few articles, maybe the first page but then they look no further. If your website isn't near the 'top of Google' then it isn't working as hard as it could for you. This is where SEO comes into the equation.

Email Marketing –

People seem to forget about this one, but it used to be a primary method of marketing for many companies. It has worked very well for me in the past, and still does now. It allows you to contact existing customers, as well as potential ones, directly to their inbox by sending them newsletters or updates that they may be interested in. It can be a bit of a slow process, but if done regularly, it will remind people who you are and what you do. When I first started developing our export business, I used this method and it had a great effect. I had a database of around a thousand new potential customers and I sent an email out to them basically saying who we are and what we do. The enquiries started to build up and, eventually, I secured over seventy new customers, worth millions, for my company. It all started with a single email and, although it had to be done on a monthly basis in conjunction with other advertising strategies, it really paid off in the long run.

Paid Advertising

When you think of 'marketing', paid advertising is likely what first comes to your mind. There are many different platforms and methods of paid advertisements. You could, for example, take out an advert in an industry magazine or newsletter. It can feel very complicated, especially for new businesses, if you are just starting out. You'll be asking yourself, *what kind of advertisement do I need? Where should I place the advertisement?* And, probably, a million other questions. My advice is to keep it simple. Your first advertisements don't need to be anything fancy. If you're a plumber, for example, maybe the best method of advertising is in your local paper. Consider what your clients will be reading/accessing, and explore those options. The whole point of paid advertising is for your company to be visible to potential customers.

Why is Marketing Important?

This might seem self-explanatory, and it is, for the most part. Marketing is important because it brings new customers to your business. In my humble opinion, if you don't tell people about your business, you'll not sell anything. People need to know that you exist, and what you do, or you will inevitably fail. Without marketing, the pool of people you will have to sell to is essentially non-existent. When I speak to people in business, something I hear so often is that they don't have the time or the budget for marketing. Marketing can be free. It doesn't have to cost a penny, other than your time. And, without it, you're starving your business of the oxygen it needs to survive.

In a downturn, the first thing that companies seem to cut back on is their marketing budget, and this makes no sense to me. Sales are the outcome of marketing. It makes customers (both current and potential) aware of you, your products, and your services. By using a good marketing strategy, you can build trust with your customers, build a good reputation, and attract people to buy your products or use your services.

Top Five Reasons to Market

Marketing allows you to…

1. Engage with your current and future customers.
2. Create a positive brand image.
3. Increase sales.
4. Improve customer loyalty.
5. Make you, and your brand/company, known.

Top Ten Marketing Tips

You have to make marketing work for you. In order to do that, you have to have a marketing strategy that you stick to. That doesn't mean that you continue with something that isn't working. If your marketing strategy isn't doing it for you, reflect and adapt, but don't stop. Consistency is key. So, here are my top ten marketing tips to set you on the right path.

1. You have to have a website.

This is not negotiable, I'm afraid. Without a website, a business just doesn't look professional. When a person first hears about a company, in my experience, the first thing they do is check out the website. The website should tell them everything they need to know about your company and what it is you do. It should also demonstrate that you are reliable. Websites don't need to cost the earth, this is a common misconception. Of course, you can go all out and have a fancy all-singing, all-dancing website, but you don't need to. The most important thing is that you have one, and that you can direct people to it. The content should be up-to-date and relevant.

TOP TIPS: *Remember to ensure that the website is optimised for mobile phones, as most people will be accessing it from a mobile device. And, make sure that any photos/videos you use are royalty-free or your own.*

2. You have a social media presence.

Get your business on social media. You don't have to be on every platform, but I would advise that you at least have a Facebook and a LinkedIn. I would also recommend Instagram and Twitter, if you want to branch out further. Some businesses lend themselves perfectly to platforms like TikTok and YouTube too. I find that I consistently post highlights such as exhibitions, new staff, awards, local community engagement, as this helps to create a positive and authentic image of our company. Be regular with it! It can be difficult, but start slow. Maybe do a post a day, or even every couple of days, initially. Don't go hell for leather and then not post for months. This doesn't show you are reliable.

3. Videos are a great advertising tool.

I only started doing video content a few years ago, and I wish I'd done it sooner. It can be quite daunting, but it is well worth it. In today's world, most people access their content through video, so jump on that bandwagon. Keep your videos short and sweet. Captivate your audience in the first few seconds before they scroll on. Make it educational – share knowledge or advice. This builds that trust factor and shows that you are a good company to work with. Don't use video as a selling tool, use it as an engagement tool.

4. Get involved in podcasts.

Like videos, podcasts are growing in popularity. People listen to them in the car, walking the dog, eating breakfast. Business people today want to consume more and more knowledge and the easiest way to do that is via podcasts. They might seem scary at first, like videos, but it is something you get used to. Podcasts can be done as a panel or on your own, the most important thing is just to have a go. I've done a few of these now and every time they're released, I can't believe the outcome. Firstly, they highlight the great work my company is doing. Secondly, they allow me to show customers who I am and to build some element of trust. Podcasts elevate you to an expert in your field, and people will then turn to you for answers.

5. **Put people at the forefront.**

Businesses are about people. People buy from people. Some of the most memorable marketing I've seen has been because you can see the person behind it. Marketing *should* be personal. It should show who you and your team really are. Customers want to know who they're buying from and the more they know about you, the more they will trust you, and the more likely they are to buy from you. For years, people hid their staff from the limelight but times are changing and it is time to put your staff (and yourself) front and centre.

6. **Don't forget your existing customers.**

You want new customers, of course you do. But you also want to retain existing customers. Marketing is an ideal way to hold onto existing business. Sending regular emails with important and useful information (not spam) and connecting with them on social media by interacting with their content too, go a long way. You should make sure that your current customers are still in the loop and are not forgotten. You already have them through the door, continue to impress them. By looking after existing customers, they are more likely to refer people to you and shout about how great your business is. Nothing feels better than getting a new customer because of a recommendation from a current/previous customer. It means that you are doing something right.

7. **Support your local community.**

Not only is this the right thing to do, but it looks good to potential customers. This is a form of marketing. It is getting your name, and your services/products out there. It builds trust and cements your place in your local area. This is particularly important for SMEs who serve their local area in some way.

SIDE STORY: In the past, at Corrosion Resistant Materials, we have sponsored local sports teams, events, school award evenings, and given to charities. It gets your brand out there, while also supporting good causes. You can use the content created from such events on your social media/website too. In the past, I've spoken at school assemblies, taken part in career days, mentored local business people, and I currently host a networking group. All of these activities play a part in your marketing. I would also highly recommend contacting and joining your local chamber of commerce as they may run events that can help you engage with, and meet, local businesses and people. They can also help promote your business to a wider audience.

8. Focus on creating great content.

Unfortunately, you can't just post any old stuff on social media and call it a day. You should consider carefully what content you're uploading. Is it useful? Relevant? Will it support your target audience in some way? Ask yourself what they want to know and gear your content towards that. If in doubt, start by telling your story. Who is your company? Where did it come from? Who are the main faces behind it? And, don't forget, you can reuse your content in the future by repurposing or updating it. If it worked once, it will work again.

9. **Create a memorable message.**

You need people to remember you. In order to do this, you need a very clear message of who you are and what your company does. You should be able to encapsulate this in a couple of sentences, phrases, or (even better) words. You want this message to be clear and stick in people's minds. Our current message is 'STOCK, SOURCE, SUPPLY'. It's simple, catchy, and it shows what we do.

10. Research. Research. Research.

Don't go into this blind. As with all aspects of business, it is important to find out what works best for you. If you're unsure, look at your competitors or customers and see what they're doing. If it works for them, it may well work for you. Try to monitor each type of marketing that you do and use this to assess whether it is successful. Has it engaged with people? Has it brought you business? A lot of marketing can be free, but it takes time, which is also a valuable resource. Keep tabs on the number of enquiries and orders you gain from each marketing attempt. You can then see your return on investment, which is an important factor to consider when running a company.

An Example:
You might pay £1000 for a page in a trade magazine. As a result, you receive 5 enquiries and 2 orders, totalling £5,000. This is a success in my books. So then imagine what could happen if you spent £10,000 on marketing – could you get £50,000 back? You will only know if you monitor the effectiveness of your marketing.

Words of Wisdom from People Wiser than Me!

There's no point reinventing the wheel. Let me share with you some quotes that will make you stop and think about your marketing strategies.

'Stopping advertising to save money is like stopping your watch to save time.'
Henry Ford

'Don't push people to where you want to be; meet them where they are.'
Meghan Keaney Anderson VP of Marketing at HubSpot

'Good marketing makes the company look smart. Great marketing makes the customer feel smart.'
Joe Chernov

'Don't find customers for your product. Find products for your customers.'
Seth Godin

Summary

Marketing is <u>the activity of promoting and selling products or services,</u> <u>including market research and advertising.</u> In essence, it is the act of attracting <u>potential customers to a product or service.</u> It is a combination of your efforts to bring customers into your company, in addition to keeping the ones you already have. For the most part, finding what works for you and your company will be a learning curve. Whatever you choose to do, find something that you can manage and be consistent in. My advice is to prioritise your website because the majority of potential clients will make that their first stop. If you work on the SEO of it, it will also bring in potential customers too. Marketing is not something that should be overlooked. It is such a key part of ensuring that your company comes across as trustworthy and knowledgeable, as well as bringing in new customers. Marketing doesn't have to be complicated you just have to get your company's name out there in a positive way.

Three takeaways...
1. **Prioritise your website.**
2. **Utilise social media.**
3. **Monitor the success of different strategies.**

Exporting

Sending goods or services to another country for sale.

Exporting is the act of selling goods or services that are produced in one country to a person/business in another country. Without going into too much detail, exporting is incredibly important to the global economy, as it can help drive economic growth, create employment opportunities and foster international collaboration. However, in terms of you and your business, it can also support you to be successful.

What to Expect...

If you're relatively new to the business world, exporting can feel like a considerable challenge to face. And it likely will be a huge learning curve for you, but the rewards are too good to pass up. In this chapter, we'll cover...

- What Exporting Is.
- Why Exporting is Essential.
- How Exporting Can Work for You.
- My Top 10 Tips for Exporting.

What is Exporting?

We already know that exporting is the act of producing goods or services in one country and selling these goods or services in another country. The goods or services that are being sold are called 'exports'. Exporting is something that

I've been involved in for the last sixteen years so not only am I very experienced in this aspect of business, but I'm very familiar with the dos and don'ts. As a little bit of background, I started out exporting umbrella frames and some other goods to France and Spain and have, over the years, developed export markets for companies, set up export procedures, and visited with many customers around the globe. In addition, I have set up and managed export departments, developed worldwide agency networks, and have experience exporting and growing businesses in over forty different countries and markets, so it's safe to say that I know what I'm talking about when it comes to exports.

SIDE STORY: Very recently, in 2022, I received a Queen's Award for Enterprise in International Trade, something I'm exceedingly proud of. I also received a Made in Sheffield award for exporting. I have witnessed first-hand the benefit that exporting has on a business and I wholeheartedly believe it is something that can completely transform a business. Back in 2018, when I joined Corrosion Resistant Materials, exports were only a small contributor to the business. By moving a focus to exporting, we have gone from five members of staff to thirteen. We've gone from £1 million in turnover, to £5 million. We've gone from 50 customers to 400, and 30 orders per month to 100. In placing the focus on exporting, we've given the company a stable and profitable future.

Why is Exporting Essential?

It is difficult to overstate the benefits of exporting for a business, in my experience. I'm not saying that growing the exporting side of your business is going to be an easy feat, but there are so many reasons why it is beneficial to do so.

1. **Exporting enables companies to grow.**

Many companies start out selling locally. This makes sense because it can be simple to do and can be done relatively quickly. However, selling locally can limit the growth of your business as you have a smaller pool of customers. This is especially prevalent if you're selling something that's niche, as you work your way through the pool of potential customers very quickly. The way to combat this is by opening up your business to a wider area, and subsequently internationally. It makes sense that the wider you cast your net, the more potential customers you have.

An Example:

In my industry, steel stockholding, the UK is a very saturated market and there is a lot of competition. Given that the UK accounts for 1% of global sales, if you can only trade within the UK then your business is extremely limited. As you unlock more potential customers, by casting a wider net, your business has the space to grow. In my specific case, trading in the UK meant around £1-2 million in sales, but this very quickly became upwards of £5 million as we began exporting. Additionally, growth through export will also lead to more sales/growth in the UK market too.

2. Exporting protects your business from market fluctuations.

The process of exporting opens you up to so many more markets. These new markets might be within Europe, the Middle East, the Far East, the USA, Africa, etc. Many of these are emerging markets and show incredible growth in comparison to the UK. In every UK recession, those that export are considerably more likely to come out of the other side of it. Generally speaking, as one market drops, another will increase. If you only work in one market, then your business doesn't have anything to fall back on. Similarly, if your product is seasonal, as many are, exporting extends the window that your product is in demand.

3. Exporting enhances your company's profile.

The process of exporting puts your business on more people's radars. Your company profile grows across the globe as more people become familiar with it. It is thanks to exporting that I, and my company, have been given several awards. With awards comes prestige. We have been able to use this success in our marketing and have grown into an expert in the field. And customers are always drawn to companies that appear to be experts in their fields. Something to consider is that by opening your business up to exporting, you will become more desirable to larger companies who have both UK and international sites, as many companies like to use the same business across their whole international organisation.

4. Exporting creates jobs.

As your company grows, you will need to employ more staff. This, in turn, allows your company to grow further as the cycle repeats itself. Creating new jobs not only benefits your company, but also your local economy. It may result in more machinery, a bigger warehouse and, of course, more profits for you and your shareholders.

5. Exporting brings more customers.

This one is a no-brainer. The number of sales you complete, the bigger your turnover. It also spreads the risk and gives the company a stronger position in the market. If you are UK based and you only have 100 customers, for example, when a big customer stops purchasing from you, you may be in trouble. However, if you had 300 customers, and many of them were international, the loss of a customer or two, even if they're big customers, would not be as detrimental to your company. With more customers comes higher profits and less risk.

6. Exporting improves your own supply chain.

Yes, exporting increases your customer base. In doing this, it will also open up the possibility of working with more suppliers. By increasing your supply chain, you will have more options on where you buy your supplies from. Not only does this give you additional buying power, as you have a choice on where to buy your supplies, but you may also be exposed to new and innovative products that you can bring to your customers.

As you can see, there are many reasons why you should focus on exporting within your business. If you're thinking of longevity, then you have to place more emphasis on exporting.

Top Ten Tips for Exporting

Now that I've convinced you that exporting is an invaluable aspect of your business and you've decided that you want to break into the international market, let's discuss how best to approach this venture.

1. Create an export plan.

I've said it once, I'll likely say it hundreds of times in this book alone. You have to have a plan. Failing to plan is planning to fail. So, before you start exporting, you have to create an export plan. Research is key. Who are your ideal customers? Who will you target? How will you export? There are so many factors that need to be considered. But don't fear, I'll share with you how I would approach this situation.

When you begin to create an export plan, concentrate on the customers you'd like to target. Keep it small at first and maybe concentrate on one or two key companies or countries to start with, and then you can build out from there. You cannot conquer the whole world in a week or two, unfortunately. As your customer list begins to grow, so will the list of companies you export to.

TOP TIP: *As you grow your exports, you might want to consider attending overseas exhibitions and visiting international customers. However, you should be aware of the costs. A 2-3 day trip to Europe can cost around £1000, while a trip to the Middle East can easily cost four times that. Remember, you want to see growth but you also want to see profit, and spending too much time travelling can eat away at that profit. You have to weigh up the benefits of travelling and be selective.*

2. Put systems in place beforehand.

Before you do any international sale, you need to make sure that your infrastructure is set up and ready to cope with the extra pressures of exporting. You'll need to understand the paperwork required, understand different currencies, learn to pack goods correctly for air and sea freight, and understand any international law that may apply to exporting certain goods. It is essential to involve your whole operation in this effort so that everybody is aware of the additional steps required for international shipping. Knowing this from day one will make sure that you can export and that you can get the goods to customers on time, which is essential if you want to get paid quickly for your services.

3. Insure your customers.

Exporting comes with a higher risk of not getting paid. You may be dealing with companies that you have never dealt with before, or even ones you might not have heard of, and you need to guarantee that you'll get paid for your services. The way to do this is to speak to your bank or insurance company, they will then be able to add customer-specific insurance for you. This grants a credit limit that you can work to with your new customers and if you're not paid, you will be covered by the bank/insurer. If your insurer refuses to insure you for certain customers, this is a red flag. In these instances, it is worth getting payment upfront before you ship the product. You will then be paid before your product ships, and this ensures that you are paid for your products.

4. **Speak to an international transport company.**

Some export clients will want you to ship the goods to them, which is to be expected. For this, you will need a reliable and experienced transport company. A good reputable transport company will not only ship the products for you, but they will also support you with paperwork and ensure that the customer receives their goods on time. Transport companies can hold a wealth of knowledge and, following Brexit, we relied heavily on ours to keep us up to date in order to ensure that we were completing paperwork (such as export declarations, tax and duty returns, and certificates of origin) correctly. Their insider knowledge can help you to relay the correct information to your customers, which helps to ensure they have a positive experience.

5. **Build valuable relationships.**

A considerable part of exporting is getting to know your customer – learn their expectations, but also learn their culture. If you are to work with people from all over the world, you will need to be considerate of different working hours, time zones, practices, languages, and cultures. Being able to demonstrate that you are respectful will help you to form a good relationship with your customers, which in turn increases sales. As with any sales, your network is key. Once you've built a good international network, you are golden. Developing good customer relationships means that you will create more opportunities for yourself as they are more likely to refer others to you and recommend your services. If one customer recommends you to another, the new customer is far more likely to purchase from you.

6. Choose a route to market.

As part of your plan, you will need to build in *how* you want to sell. You might wonder what I'm talking about here, let me explain. At first, you'll likely be working with customers directly. But, as you grow, you might want to consider a distributor or agent. An agent is somebody who will introduce you to prospective customers and then charges a commission on the sale. A distributor will buy from you at an agreed price and then sell to their own customers.

I have successfully worked with agents over the years and, in my opinion, if you want to grow in a particular market, they can be a valuable resource. You will therefore have somebody who is local and understands where to sell, the local market, local tax and shipping considerations, etc. You need to be aware that while working with an agent can be a huge asset, it is important that you work with the right one. You want an agent who will put your company first and will add value to what you're doing (and what you can do) in that particular region. When approaching an agent, try to get a recommendation and always do it on a trial period first. If it works, great. If it doesn't, move on, no harm done.

7. Understanding Incoterms

Incoterms are a set of internationally recognised rules which set out the responsibilities of buyers and sellers. They specify who is responsible for paying for and managing the shipment, documentation, insurance, customer clearance, etc. Familiarising yourself with these eleven rules and regulations helps you to avoid any nasty surprises and unexpected costs. You can get all of this information online and there are even courses that you can complete to help you understand everything you need to know.

8. Contact your local Chamber of Commerce and Department of International Trade

If you are new to exporting, your local Chamber of Commerce can be a huge help. They can give you advice, check you have everything you need in place, and can even put you in contact with companies who are already exporting. Seeking advice as support is critical to successfully exporting. Learning from others who are more experienced can make all the difference, especially if you had somebody you can reach out to for advice should any issues arise. Your local Department of International Trade can also be a great support as you begin to venture into exporting. Not only do they offer advice, but they also run trade missions where you can go to another country with a group of local businesses and visit exhibitions and meet with local businesses. They can help you with grants and funding too, which can be difficult to navigate alone. As a company, we have used several grants and funding through the DIT and this has allowed us to visit customers, exhibit at trade shows, and has assisted with marketing.

9. Speak to your local university about market research.

Many universities can assist you with market research. They have business schools that will take your idea and produce detailed market research plans that may include who to contact, information about competitors, and different routes to market. The best thing is that this is free. If you were to pay for this type of research it would cost thousands of pounds. It's a resource that many businesses don't know about and can be very useful when you're breaking into the export arena.

10. Make the most of technology.

I'm showing my age here, but nowadays it is far easier to speak and interact with customers all over the world than ever before. Teams and Zoom meetings have become so common, particularly since the pandemic. Email and WhatsApp (which is very popular in the Middle and Far East) are both free, and you can do this at any time of day. If you do plan on speaking on video chat or over the phone then remember to take into consideration the time difference. When I first started exporting, the only way to speak to customers was over the phone, and this meant a lot of late nights and early mornings.

Words of Wisdom from People Wiser than Me!

You all know the drill by now. So, here we go, words of wisdom on exporting from people who said something that I think you'll all benefit from having read.

"Exporting is an act of courage that creates value."
Oscar Saenz

"Success is a process, not a destination."
Zig Ziglar

"Exporting is a powerful engine of economic growth."
Christine Lagarde

"Exporting is a force multiplier for creating jobs."
John Kerry

Summary

Exporting is the act of selling goods or services that are produced in one country to a person/business in another country. It can feel like a huge challenge, and that's because it is. Most things in life that are worth doing are difficult and exporting is no exception. Exporting comes as a considerable learning curve, there are so many factors that you need to familiarise yourself with and get right. Putting in the effort to research, learn and ask for advice at the start of your journey will see you right. Remember, by opening your business up for export you are making yourself available to so many more customers, protecting your company from market fluctuations, and setting your company on the path for growth. If you take my advice, you won't go far wrong.

Three Takeaways
1. **Research, plan, and prepare.**
2. **Make the most of technology.**
3. **Your local Chamber of Commerce and DIT are invaluable resources.**

Business Development

The process of implementing strategies and opportunities across your organisation to promote growth and boost revenue.

Generating new business is a crucial part of any organisation. The creation of new opportunities allows your business to grow financially. This, in turn, enables you to grow in physical size and to take on new staff. For any new business, all business is new business. However, as you continue to grow, it is fundamental that you keep this pipeline open and expanding, making sure that you continue to generate new opportunities for you and your business. The key to a successful business is always looking at opportunities to develop further, as this prevents you from stagnating.

What to Expect...

We all know that we should be developing our businesses. As a business owner, we all want our businesses to be bigger and better, to go from strength to strength. However, knowing that you should be undertaking business development and knowing how to do it are two different things. In this chapter, we will cover...

- What Business Development Is
- Why Business Development is Essential for Any Company
- My Top Ten Tips for Business Development Success

What is Business Development?

Business development is the process of implementing strategies and opportunities across your organisation in order to promote growth and boost revenue. It encompasses all of the actions you take in order to further expand and strengthen your business. In basic terms, it is the act of engaging with new customers and encouraging them to place orders with your business. However, when thinking about business development, your sights should be set on long-term gains rather than short-term sales. You want to encourage the customers to purchase from you over and over again, not just once. Bringing in new customers can be challenging, but if you do it systematically and correctly, you will develop a good relationship with them and they will continue to buy from you into the future.

By looking systematically at business development, growth will come naturally. For example, if you are a new business, in months 1 and 2 you may have 5 new customers each month. If those customers all buy from you in month 2, you will have 10 customers that month. If you continue to gain around 5 new customers each month, the number of customers you have accumulates and snowballs. As a result, each month you will see growth.

An Example:

When I joined Corrosion Resistant Materials in 2018, we wanted to grow our customer base in the export market. We had no customers in this market initially, but within the first year, we had over 50 customers in total, with 30 of these customers buying continually each month. This gave us a strong platform from which to continue to grow and develop.

Why is Business Development Essential?

In my experience, business development is the main thing any business needs to focus on in order to remain successful (or become successful). There are four key benefits of business development, all of which can have a considerable impact on your company.

1. The generation of new sales.

Every single business needs to sell in order to survive. If you don't sell, you don't have a business. Even more established businesses need to generate new business avenues to maintain (and increase) the turnover and profit revenues they've established. They need to replace business that may have been lost to competition and customers who simply don't require the product they're selling anymore, perhaps because they've gone out of business themselves. To simply rely on your current customer base is dangerous. Although it can be tempting to rely on your existing customer base, if you are not bringing in new customers each month, then you run the risk of stagnating and you will consequently see a drop in revenue.

TOP TIP: *It is important to not have more than 5% of your business with one customer. I have known some businesses close overnight because they'd become overly reliant on one customer to keep them afloat.*

2. The creation of long-term value for your company.

By growing your business the right way, and by adopting a strategic approach to business development that puts the customer at the heart of it, you will create long-term growth and success. Longevity is a goal for all businesses, and this strategic approach to business development helps to protect you against challenges you may face in the future. The more customers you have, particularly repeat customers, the more stable the foundation of your business is. This is the foundation upon which you can build and grow.

3. The improvement of your company's image.

The way in which your business is perceived by others is a considerable factor in the success of any business. By focusing on the fundamentals of business development you can make your company a problem-solver in your field. You can ensure that your brand is seen in the right places and by the right people. Creating an image that you are a helpful, knowledgeable market-leader, through the implementation of a solid business development plan, puts you on the map and ensures that your business is seen in the correct light.

4. Support to move into new markets.

If part of your plan is to move into new areas, business development will provide the backbone for this. You might be heavily involved in one very specific area, for example, but feel you can move into a new area to help grow your business and reduce the risks associated with being heavily involved in only one area of the market. By adopting a business development strategy for moving into the new area, you will be able to systematically and effectively move into that area and continue to grow.

The benefits of implementing strategic business development within your business are incredibly varied, and the outcome can be entirely specific to your niche and areas you feel you need to develop further. At the end of the day, business development boils down to reducing risk and ensuring the longevity of your business. Having the ability to step back and assess how best to move forward with business development can be difficult as we can often find looking at our own business objectively near-impossible. This, like most things in life, comes with practise and experience. I've been lucky enough to be involved in business development strategies for both Corrosion Resistant Materials, and also in previous roles. In my experience, I've picked up some tips along the way that will help you get started.

Top Ten Tips for Business Development

We're going to keep it simple and to the point. Here are the top ten tips you need to consider when you're starting to establish a business development strategy.

1. Define your growth targets.

How will you know whether you're successful if you don't have goals to aim for? First and foremost, you need to set targets for your business. This might be the number of new clients you'd like to gain, revenue you want to make, or profit you want to achieve each month. Knowing your current numbers will support you to create these targets, as will knowing where you want to go. A clear picture of what you want to achieve will support you in putting the right steps in place. It is important to remember to review and adapt your plan (the steps you put in place) each month and adapt where needed. If something doesn't seem to be having the impact you thought it would, then adapt and try something different.

An Example:

You might currently have a turnover of £1 million and have 50 customers. You want to grow your business to £1.5 million in the next year and in order to do this, you'd need 75 customers. This equates to 25 new customers in total, with approximately 2 new customers per month.

2. Decide who your ideal customer is.

If you have an image in your head of what your ideal customer is, it can make it far easier to ensure that you're targeting the right potential customers. Consider this, you already have several customers, why do they buy from you? What type of business are they? Do they have something in common with one another? Once you identify what your ideal customer is, you'll have more clarity about which companies to set your sights on. If we consider Corrosion Resistant Materials, our best customers are the ones who buy a large array of different grades of materials. They may want heat treatment as well as machining, and they like a supplier who can offer that full service. Once I had this profile in mind, I could find similar companies or buyers who fitted this model. If they did, then my chance of successfully selling to them was a lot higher.

3. Find where your ideal customers are.

Once you already know what your ideal customer looks like, and you've established some growth targets, you need to find out where your ideal customers are. Industry networking events and exhibitions, which we discussed earlier, are often a great place to start, but you may also want to look at local trade associations. We are members of the BSSA (British Stainless Steel Association), BVAA (British Valve and Actuators Association) and Made in Yorkshire. All three of these associations have around 200 members each, many of whom I could class as our 'ideal customer'. The associations put on events where I can meet the other members and discuss how we could help them. By being part of these organisations, we have generated new business, and achieved our previous business development goals.

TOP TIP: *If you join trade associations, you need to attend events and be active in order to get your desired results. It can take time. However, if you persist it will pay off. Remember, a strong network is key to business growth.*

It is also worth looking at where your ideal customers go to find out information. This could be social media or certain publications. If you 'show up' in the places they are looking for information, they are more likely to engage with you, therefore bringing in new customers and business.

4. Be systematic in your approach.

Once you know who you want to target (potential ideal customers you have identified), you want to adopt a systematic approach. Don't just go blindly contacting everyone all the time. This won't achieve the results you are looking for and will waste your time. It is important to categorise each potential customer and lead into the following stage of the buying process, as this will inform you of what approach to take.

- **Suspect** - people who are interested in what you sell, but may not have the budget or need to buy from you.
- **Prospect** – your ideal customer. They are buying what you currently sell. You have qualified them and they may have the budget, the authority and the requirement to purchase from you.
- **Lead** – prospects who are engaging with you. They have sent an enquiry and may now be ready to buy.
- **Buyer** – has already bought from you.
- **Customer** – people buying from you on a regular basis and are the cornerstones of your business.

The key is to move each potential customer along in this process from one category to the next, and to engage with each group in a different way. How you treat a suspect and a customer will be vastly different, for example, as they require different input from you. Remember, once a suspect becomes a customer you still have to work hard to keep it that way or they may slip back down the funnel again. It is also really important that as a company, and with one eye on business development, you continue to gain suspects to pop into the top of the funnel. Without a new stream, your customers will soon dry up. It's a continuous effort and cycle to keep customers engaged while also bringing in new buyers and hopefully turning them into customers.

5. Keep track of your business development.

Keeping track of your business development allows you to monitor your success and to assess what is working and what isn't. Once you've embarked on your business development journey, and have a systematic approach in place, it is important to create a record of what you are doing, with whom, and where they are on their sales journey. It can be something as simple as a basic spreadsheet. It needs to tell you who you contacted, your contact with them, and where they are in their buying journey. The simple categories outlined above will be useful to track their progress.

6. Keep on top of it.

I know that this is often easier said than done, but it is really easy to forget about planning for the future as you get busy. Daily tasks such as order processing, invoicing and ensuring goods are despatched on time are all fundamental aspects of your business and can find themselves at the top of your list of priorities. However, without one eye on business development, you will struggle to grow and you may see your business turnover decline with time, which is obviously something to be avoided. Anything is better than nothing, and consistency is the way to go. Even if you just do a little each day or week, it will pay off in the long-term. So many businesses make the mistake of only focusing on business development in the lean times, when it's quiet, but it needs to become a part of how you consistently run your business. Don't let business development fall by the wayside, it's your safety net should difficult times come.

7. Consider other market sectors.

You have already established what your ideal customer looks like, but perhaps there are others from different industries or sectors that you haven't considered yet. Diversifying helps you to spread the risk, especially if one market sector goes into decline. If you are able to expand into other sectors, the risk decreases. In other words, you don't have all your eggs in one basket. It's the same principle we mentioned earlier when discussing increasing the number of customers you have.

An Example:

At Corrosion Resistant Materials, we had over 90% of our customers based in the oil and gas sector. This left us vulnerable to declines in this sector and so we diversified into aerospace manufacturing, power generation, defence, and renewables. We were still selling the same material to the same type of buyers, but doing so in different sectors. This helped to spread out the risk. Diversifying will likely involve a lot of time and research but it will be well worth it.

8. Focus on marketing.

We've already covered marketing in great detail, so you know how to get started with that. In the context of business development, by knowing who your ideal customers are and where you can locate them, you can adapt your marketing strategy in line with this. Having a targeting marketing approach will reap the rewards long-term and bring in new potential customers to the top of your sales funnel.

9. Prioritise the needs of your customer.

You should never focus on 'selling'. When pushing for new business, it is really easy to fall into the trap of selling what your company does. Instead, you should learn more about your prospects. What do they need? Where do they buy from? If you understand their pain points, you will be able to offer solutions from your company, rather than pushing for a sale. Listen to and qualify your suspects, seize the opportunities that present themselves. Developing long-term relationships is a considerable asset for any business.

An Example:

I know a suspect buys 316 Stainless and they buy from a competitor of ours. They have a really good service and a long history. The chance of them changing suppliers is very slim. However, they also buy other materials too, so I try to understand which materials they're struggling with. If they say, as an example, that they're struggling to find Alloy 800 and it is impacting their business, I can seize this opportunity and offer them a solution to their problem. If I do this, I am more likely to turn them into a customer.

10. Persevere.

Don't give up. Bringing in new customers to any business isn't easy and at times it can be incredibly frustrating. You might work extremely hard on one prospect, get them talking and enquiring only for them to go elsewhere at the 11th hour. You need to persevere and keep the faith. Don't let a 'no' knock you back. Persistence and dedication to your business development plan will provide you with results in the end. See it as a marathon, not a sprint. If you continue to do the right things and remain consistent, then you will reap the rewards in the end. Some of my customers, I had been tracking for years before we eventually found a way to work together. Remember, people buy from people and if you keep showing up and offering solutions to people, you will eventually find a way for them to say 'yes' to what you're offering.

Words of Wisdom from People Wiser than Me!

Here we go again. Now that you've heard my wisdom on this topic, let's take a look at the wisdom of others.

'Business opportunities are like buses, there's always another one coming.'
Richard Branson

'The minute you're satisfied with where you are, you aren't there anymore.'
Tony Gwynn

'Failure is not to be feared. It is from failure that most growth comes.'

Dee Hock

Summary

<u>Business development is the process of implementing strategies and opportunities across your organisation to promote growth and boost revenue.</u> If you're not pursuing the development of your business, then you open yourself up to a considerable risk. The key ways to reduce risk within a business is through bringing in more customers and diversifying, and business development is how you do that. It can often get lost by the wayside and replaced by the daily tasks on your to-do list, but you should always be scheduling time for business development. Whether twenty minutes each day, or a couple of hours each week, it all adds up. A systematic approach to business development helps you to keep track of what is working for you and what isn't. It supports you in remembering which potential customers you're already in contact with and where they sit in your categories. Nothing worth doing is ever easy, but at least following a systematic plan for business development can make it as simple as possible. The rewards of business development are often the longevity and safety of your business, so it is well worth taking the time to get it right.

Three Takeaways

1. **Be systematic and consistent.**

2. **Decide on your 'ideal customer'.**

3. **Explore other sectors.**

Building Your Personal Brand

The construction and promotion by an individual of their own public image, often done through social media.

We can all agree that building a strong brand is important for any company. Your branding tells the world about who your company is and what you do. It communicates your ethos, your unique character and, hopefully, creates a positive perception of your company. Now, that being said, for most sales professionals, this falls naturally into place as we focus on providing a high-quality service/product for our customers. However, in my experience, branding needs to be a conscious effort. You have to work to create an image of your company that mirrors who you are and what you do. Something to consider, which I think is incredibly important and is often widely forgotten, is that branding should be personal. People buy from people, we know that. A buyer wants to feel connected with who they are buying from on a personal level. They want to build trust, a relationship and, above all else, feel invested in the whole buying/sales process.

What to Expect...

Branding doesn't have to be hugely complicated, but thought and care should go into creating a positive image of your company so that potential buyers feel connected with you, in some way. This is where the personal side of branding comes in. In this chapter, we will cover...

- What Personal Branding Is
- Why Personal Branding is Essential
- My Top Ten Tips for Creating a Personal Brand

What is Personal Branding?

If you've been in business for any amount of time, you'll hear the word 'branding' left, right and centre. Branding is key to creating the right perception of your company. In my experience, for branding to have the biggest impact, it has to be personal. Potential buyers need to know exactly who you are and what you stand for. In my opinion, many sales professionals, although they are good at selling a product, are not as good at selling themselves. Instead of promoting themselves and the value of what they are doing, they will focus on a single product or service. Telling the world who you are and what you do is your 'personal brand', essentially it is the human being behind a business. A personal brand is the unique combination of skills and experiences that make you who you are. It is what makes you unique and sets you apart from everybody else.

You may have come across the term 'personal branding' many times before. It's been a bit of a buzzword in recent years, especially in sales training courses and on social media. You might think that it's a waste of time, or a fad, but more and more sales professionals are creating their own personal brand and image and I believe that it is here to stay. I first started creating my own personal brand during the lockdown in 2020. For me, it was all about showing the world who I was, what I had achieved, and what made me different from all the other sales professionals out there.

Why is Personal Branding Important?

Before you embark on the journey into personal branding, it is essential to understand exactly why it is worth your time. After all, we're all busy people and business pulls our time in many different ways. So, here is why I think personal branding is important.

1. **Standing out from the crowd.**

Personal branding supports you to stand out from the crowd. Today, more than ever, in the business world, we need to rise above our competition and set ourselves apart from everybody else. Most sales professionals know that it is important to do this for any company, to focus on unique selling points and the public perception of the business. They find a niche or product that is different to everything else out there, and this drives business their way. The process is no different for personal branding. The branding you do for a business, can (and should) also be done for an individual. It is important to tell everybody out there what makes you different and why they should approach you, rather than all the other salespeople out there. People remember those who stand out from the crowd and your personal branding, your public image, communicates clearly who you are and what you do.

2. **More opportunities.**

Personal branding will bring in more opportunities for your company. People will associate you with your company and, if your personal branding is effective, it will bring in more customers. But it doesn't just end there. Personal branding will also create more opportunities for you, as an individual. The better the perception is of you, and the more 'known' you are, could be the difference between securing new customers for your business and even obtaining a new career opportunity. There's also a chance that you may be approached to do things you might never have dreamed of. For me, it has brought growth for myself and my company and, through promoting myself and my personal brand, I have won several industry awards, for myself and my company, and this has ensured sustained growth.

3. **Trust, influence, authority and professional relationships.**

Personal branding facilitates the growth of good, solid professional relationships. If people feel like they know you, they are more likely to engage with you. Through the development of your own personal brand, everybody can see who you are and what you stand for. People get to know you even before they meet you and when they do finally meet you, it feels like they already know you. You have already provided them with a good first impression of who are and therefore you have a solid foundation to build upon.

4. **Shows you as an expert in your field.**

Personal branding is essentially showing off what you are capable of (as well as what you stand for and your achievements). You should be sharing your personal experience and skills. If shaped in the right way, and consistently, you can come across as the go-to person for advice in your line of work. As, at the moment, not everybody has a personal brand, those who need advice are far more likely to turn to somebody they feel they know and respect. Being visible and creating your own brand means that others know exactly who you are. Imagine walking into a room at a networking event and everybody already knows who you are because you created a personal brand that works. The personal brand, in this case, works as an icebreaker for you. There's no need for introductions or small talk. Since building my own personal brand, this is very much the case for me when I go to events and I, therefore, feel far more confident meeting people, because the likelihood is that they will recognise me and I will recognise them too because I got to know them through their brand and social media presence.

5. Brings you joy.

Not only is personal branding particularly great at bringing in new customers and opportunities, but it is also fun too. I love working on personal branding. Building your own brand and creating more opportunities will enable you to meet people and do more diverse things in your working life. Others will contact you to do events, speaking opportunities, and maybe even conferences if they see you as the 'expert' you are. Over the last three years, I've been invited to do podcasts, TV/newspaper interviews, run networking events, join committees, chair roundtable discussions, join trade association boards and speak at events, all of this because I pushed myself onto social media and created my own personal brand.

The benefits of personal branding are clear. It can be quite a daunting experience initially, it can make you feel quite exposed and self-conscious, but it doesn't have to be that way. You can ease yourself into the process and make it work for you.

Top 10 Tips for Personal Branding

Here are my top tips to ensure you are successful and make the most of personal branding. It doesn't have to be a huge time-consuming task. You can make it fit easily around your work day. And, you never know, you might even enjoy it.

1. Get Online

Getting started is as simple as setting up LinkedIn, Facebook and Twitter profiles and making sure that you use them. Put a good picture on there that shows yourself in the best light and make your page stand out by adding videos, photos and articles. This is your profile so make sure it reflects you and the image you want to portray, not just your company. This is your chance to show your personality, your experiences and your skills. This is how people will get to know you, so make sure you make it count. If you want further ideas, please feel free to connect with me on LinkedIn to see a real-life example of how it is done.

2. Be Genuine

If you're not genuine, people will see through that. Share what you do online, but also share your vulnerabilities and thoughts on subjects that are relevant to you and your industry. While this is a chance to showcase what you can do, don't be boastful or make up stories. A genuine and honest approach to personal branding is the way to go. Tell the world who you are and don't feel the need to over-elaborate or exaggerate. If you do, when people meet you in person, they'll be disappointed and that is the last thing you want because the trust will instantly break down.

TOP TIP: *As tempting as it can be, don't copy other people's ideas. By being yourself, you'll instantly be original. Remember, there's nobody else out there with your exact experience, skillset and personality. Let this work in your favour.*

3. Tell Your Story

People will be more inclined to engage with you if you become a great storyteller. By that, I mean creating interesting content that others will find appealing. I don't mean you should tell lies and embellish the truth. Just tell your story as is and the right audience will come to you. For me, this looks like posting what I am doing, what events I've been to, my views and opinions on certain topics, and really anything that I think others might find interesting. I like to share the latest book I've read, what I think about certain courses, my opinion on apprenticeships, or even my views on Brexit. By talking about yourself and your views, you will create instant and meaningful connections.

As you begin telling your story and sharing your experience, consider who you are, as personal branding can be a great reflective experience.

4. Be Consistent

I'm always talking about consistency because consistency is important in so many different aspects of business (and your personal life). Creating any brand, especially your own personal brand, takes time. You need to post regularly so that everybody knows who you are and what you do. The brand, the image and the perception of you will build and develop the more content you put out there. Some try to post something daily, which is hard work, but a really good way to get started. My own approach is to post every time I do something different or noteworthy – especially if this something is positive. Networking events, winning awards, etc, are all great things to post about and create a brand image that shows you to be a professional and trustworthy individual. Commenting on other posts consistently is also an ideal way to build your personal brand. This shows what kind of content you follow and you can often add your voice to important debates without having to create your own post.

5. Don't Be Afraid to Fail

The only way you can truly fail is if you don't try. Just have a go and see what happens. Far too often people think something is an awesome idea, but get caught up doing other things. It doesn't take long at all for you to create accounts on a few social media platforms, and even if you only post a few times a week, it is better than nothing. It all adds up in the end. If you're honest with yourself and post about things that you are passionate about, then you can't fail at it. The whole point of personal branding is to show the world who you are, so just start posting and be true to yourself.

6. Be Helpful

People remember those who have helped them. Often, the best way to come across as helpful is to actually help people. I often recommend other people and businesses that we have worked with so others can reach out to them. Imagine how you would feel to know that somebody recommended you to somebody else. You would instantly build a bond with that person and be more likely to work with them in the future. Through collaboration, you will see how positively people will talk about you and how often they start to turn to you.

7. Grow Your Network

Networking is crucial for any business, but it is also an important part of personal branding. Personally, I believe it gives you more opportunities and by extending your network, you will come across people from many different backgrounds and fields who you may be able to support with their journey, or who may be able to support you with yours. The larger your network, the more people become aware of you and, therefore, the more people see your personal brand. You need to network regularly and effectively. Connect with people on a regular basis on your social media, particularly people whom you admire. The more connections you have, the more people will see (or hear) what you have to say. This will build your brand a lot quicker. A current statistic shows that 85% of jobs are filled as a direct result of networking, either in person or online.

8. Use Different Forms of Media

Varying your content is key if you're going to stand apart from the crowd. Some people prefer the written word, others prefer videos, some prefer podcasts. Utilising all types of media in your content will ensure that the most people can access it. Therefore, it is important that you build a true personal brand that involves all forms of media. In this past year, I have really stepped up my social media presence and personal branding. I regularly post photos, videos and podcasts on social media so that more people interact with, and gain something from, my content, this creates an initial bond.

9. Get Involved

In order to create great content that people want to interact with, you have to have something to say. Making sure that you're regularly attending events, conferences, exhibiting and getting involved in your local community can give you a lot of great content to share. Whatever interests you and is important to you will often be of value to others. The more you get involved in, the more you'll have to discuss, the quicker (and more effectively) your personal brand will develop.

Some Examples:
In the last three years, I have done a lot more 'activities' outside of the office. I've attended school career days, had booths at trade shows, joined trade associations, presented at conferences, appeared on podcasts, applied for awards, amongst other things. This is all with the aim of pushing myself, and my company, into the limelight. It is always easier to create positive content

when you are doing lots of varied things. If all you do is go to work and come home each day, you'll likely struggle for things to post/talk about.

10. Continue to Reinvent Your Personal Brand

The person you are today will be different to the person you are this time next year. Or in five years, or ten years. It is important to reflect to the outside world who you are at each point in time and if you have a website, or social media accounts, that don't reflect who you currently are, then you need to make it a priority to rectify this. Seeing growth, reflection and change within a person or a company shows that they are genuine and trustworthy. Nobody stays the same forever, so why should your personal brand? Being consistent, trustworthy and genuine means that you will remain current.

As you can see, creating a personal brand doesn't mean that you need to move mountains. The key is putting yourself out there and being consistent, genuine and helpful. Hopefully, you can see that little and often is better than nothing at all or posting irregularly. The more consistent you are, the easier and quicker it will be for people to form a connection with you. Connections mean opportunities. And opportunities mean growth (personally or in your company).

Words of Wisdom from People Wiser than Me!

You know what to expect by now. When I think of personal branding, and why it is imperative, these are the quotes that come to mind. You'll notice a couple of wildcard names in there, but their points are valid, so just bear with me.

'Your brand is what people say about you when you're not in the room.'
Jeff Bezos

'Today you are you! That is truer than true! There is no one alive who is you-er than you!'
Dr Seuss

'Be yourself, Everyone Else is already taken.'
Oscar Wilde

'If people like you they will listen to you, but if they trust you, they'll do business with you.'
Zig Ziglar

Summary

Personal branding is the construction and promotion by an individual of their own public image, often done through social media. Your personal brand is the image of yourself that you put out into the world. People buy from people, I've said it once, I'll say it a million times. People like to know who is behind the business and it is worth taking advantage of this, because why wouldn't you? It is so easy to create a personal brand that reflects who you genuinely are. Sharing your experience, your opinions and your values helps to create genuine connections while simultaneously bringing in more people to your network and business. Personal branding is your place to shine. It's your chance to tell your story and show people who you truly are. You don't need to spend hours and hours doing it. A daily post, or even every other day, as long as you're consistent, to build up a big picture of your personal brand, goes a long way. It benefits you and your business, and can be as simple as commenting on others' posts, sharing articles and content, and posting photos/videos of what you're up to.

Three Takeaways
1. **Be consistent**
2. **Be genuine**
3. **Be helpful**

The Power of LinkedIn

LinkedIn, launched in 2003, is a business and employment-focused social media platform.

There are many different social media platforms out there today. Social media, for better or for worse, has taken over our lives. Facebook, Twitter, YouTube, Instagram, LinkedIn, and many others, continue to grow in popularity. Businesses nowadays need to get on the social media bandwagon in order to keep up with their competition. For me, in business, the most important and widely used social media platform is LinkedIn. For a lot of people, LinkedIn gets left by the wayside in exchange for other more 'popular' platforms. If you're not utilising LinkedIn, you're missing out.

What to Expect...

Like all social media platforms, LinkedIn requires a learning curve if you're not already used to it. There are certain things you can do, and understand, to make your LinkedIn transformation more successful. The platform has over 875 million members across over 200 different countries. The majority of these members are business people and companies, and the reach of LinkedIn grows year upon year. Today, it is viewed by many, myself included, as the number one social media platform for business. In this chapter, we will cover...

- What LinkedIn Is
- Why LinkedIn is Essential for You and Your Company
- How to Create a Great LinkedIn Profile

- My Top Tips for Using LinkedIn

What is LinkedIn?

Let's start with the basics, if you've never been on LinkedIn before, it might feel a little overwhelming. I kind of think of it as the Facebook of business. According to the LinkedIn FAQs, it is, *"the world's largest professional network on the internet. You can use LinkedIn to find the right job or internship, connect and strengthen professional relationships, and learn the skills you need to succeed in your career… A complete LinkedIn profile can help you connect with opportunities by showcasing your unique professional story through experience, skills, and education…You can also use LinkedIn to organize offline events, join groups, write articles, post photos and videos, and more."*

It is also important to consider that…
- 80% of B2B sales leads come from LinkedIn
- Engagement on LinkedIn has increased 50% year on year
- It has 9 billion content impressions every week

In my experience, there are those who love LinkedIn and use it all the time (me!), those who hate it and don't see the importance of the platform, and those who would like to use it, but are not sure how. Hopefully, this chapter will alleviate some of your concerns about the platform, and show you the best way to make the most of it.

Why is LinkedIn Important?

LinkedIn is important for you as an individual, as well as your company. I first started on LinkedIn back in 2016 and since then it has been an imperative aspect of my business. LinkedIn can...

- Create awareness and promote your brand/your company/yourself.

In addition to personal pages for individual business people, LinkedIn offers a company page where you can attract followers who might be interested in what you do. Using your company-specific page, you can tell your audience (who may be current or ideal customers) any company news or developments, such as new staff, new stock ranges, and the ways you can support them. You can do this daily, weekly or monthly. My personal preference is to update the page as much as possible as the information you put on there is directly passed to those who want to see it.

- Support researching competitors and their employees.

We all do it, so there's no point in pretending we don't. We all think about what our competitors are doing and, as business leaders, we're always thinking about what other business leaders are doing. This helps us to learn and develop. LinkedIn is a great way to see this firsthand. You can check competitors' pages and see what they're doing in the marketplace. As a business, this will help you to grow and innovate new ways to stand out, be different, or offer something else to the market.

- Allow you to research customers and qualify leads.

In order to be successful in sales, we have to engage with our customers and understand their needs. There is no better way to do this, in my opinion, than through LinkedIn. By following them, you can see firsthand what makes them tick and, most importantly, what issues they're having that you can support them with. You can also use it as an amazing marketing research tool and find out all about your target companies. You can qualify companies and people within minutes and really see if they are worth pursuing. Imagine all this information and power all on one platform.

- Source and engage top talent.

Just like you target companies you want to work with, you can use LinkedIn to look for, and target, new members of staff. You can engage with them and check out their work history, see what they're like as individuals and what their achievements have been. It helps you to qualify people who have applied for a job with you and make sure that, even before the interview, they're the right person for the role.

- Improve your ranking on search engines.

Google and other search engines will rank LinkedIn company pages and posts highly. So, if you have a page and post to it regularly, it will often surface at the top of Google when people are searching. If you create SEO-based content about your business, this will help drive people to your business and to you.

- Organises contacts in one place.

As a business person, or company, we often have lists and lists of customers, and those in our pipelines. Maybe your contacts are in spreadsheets, on business cards, CRMs, etc. LinkedIn allows you to keep your contacts in one place, safely and electronically, so that they follow you around wherever you go. You can also keep up to date with all your contacts and when they move company, or you do, you never lose touch.

- It's free!

The best part of it is that this is all free. There is a paid-for version of LinkedIn (LinkedIn Premium) which gives you additional features, but the free version is definitely enough for most people and gives them access to a whole world of business opportunities. You've got nothing to lose by giving it a try.

How to Create a Great Profile

Now you know the benefits of LinkedIn, you're hopefully raring to create a profile and get using it. If you already have a profile on LinkedIn, this is your chance to assess whether it is up to scratch and make any edits you feel are necessary. I bet, by the end of this section, you'll want to give your profile a complete overhaul. You have to consider how you're going to stand out over the other 875 million users, which isn't easy. My honest opinion would be to treat it as a modern-day live CV. Tell the world who you are and how you can help them. Don't just make it solely about your company, personalise it so that it reflects you. Today, around 73% of people use their LinkedIn profile instead of a CV when they're applying for jobs. Here's how to make the best of it...

1. Choose the right profile picture.

Straight off the bat, this is the first thing people see. It clearly needs to show you and your face. It needs to be current, professional, and please try to smile. Mine is currently me recording a podcast. I'm facing the camera, laughing, and wearing branded clothing. It ticks all of the boxes for a good, professional, profile picture.

2. Add a background photo.

LinkedIn gives you the opportunity to add a background photo, in addition to your cover photo. This is an ideal way to grab people's attention. You could use a warehouse shot, product information, or, as I do, your company logo. Again, make it count as this is one of the first things people will see when they connect with you. For me, I have used the Corrosion Resistant Materials logo as it is bold and it communicates what I am most associated with. This also promotes my company and drives people to it.

3. Make good use of your headline.

Don't just use your job title, as tempting as this might be. Tell people more about yourself and how you can help them. You could list your main accomplishments, awards or achievements. If you're not sure where to start, take a look at others in a similar field or people in your network. Don't copy them, that should go without saying, but use them to get some ideas of what might work for you.

4. Tell your story and build your personal brand.

In the last chapter, we discussed the importance of building a personal brand, LinkedIn is the perfect opportunity to do that. Rather than using your summary to list all your professional qualities, use it to tell your story. Make it interesting and personal. It is your space to tell people all about you, what makes you tick, why you do what you do, and how you can support others.

5. List your relevant skills.

You are given a list of relevant skills, scroll through it and identify which ones apply to you, be careful not to overdo it though. Choose the ones that are relevant and core to who you are and what you do. By adding these, others can endorse you for these skills and within no time at all, you can portray yourself as the expert you are.

6. Use the featured post function.

Once you get posting and build up a bank of them, you can select the most important ones that reflect you and/or your company. These will remain at the top of your profile for everyone to see, so even if the posts are from months ago, they'll still be found quickly by the people you're connecting with. Things such as company videos, presentations, podcasts, posts about awards, all of these are great to showcase as a featured post. In order to do this, you will need to turn on 'creator mode', which will open up other features such as analytics, LinkedIn Live, and Newsletter.

7. Promote your experience.

The experience section is where you need to, you guessed it, write all your relevant experience. Remember, this may be seen by potential employers and by people who may want to work with you and so by highlighting your experience, you can share what you know and your background. Also, include here any organisations you have volunteered for, boards you have been on, and organisations you have supported. Don't be afraid of a long list here – if it is relevant, it is important, so list it.

8. Give recommendations.

These will show on your profile and reflect the type of person you are. It is important to give recommendations, and therefore you will also receive recommendations back. Also, don't be afraid to ask for them back, they can act as referees and show the kind of person you are to work with.

9. Profile your profile.

Check out what others see when they go to your page on LinkedIn. How can you make it better? Who are you connected with? What might others think of your page? You can't effectively evaluate your LinkedIn page, without looking at it from an outsider's perspective.

10. Complete your profile.

Make sure all sections are completed. This will ensure that the LinkedIn algorithm rewards you and promotes your posts above others with weaker profiles. You can even go as high as 'All-Star' and really stand out from the crowd. A poor incomplete profile also doesn't look good to potential new employers or clients.

Now you know how to make a great, stand-out LinkedIn profile, but how do you make it successful?

Top Ten Tips for LinkedIn Success

There are ten very simple tips that can make your LinkedIn profile work for you. I'm sure you can guess what one or two of them might be because certain things are good practice in all areas of your business.

1. Consistency is key.

Did you guess that one? In order for your LinkedIn to be successful, you have to post regularly and be consistent. Most individuals and companies will see an increase in business if they post every day. It isn't easy to do, so my advice would be to aim for consistency instead. You're better to do one post per week every week, than do ten posts in one week and none for a month.

TOP TIP: *Diarise your posts and schedule them so you do them regularly. If you're able to find the time to post daily, go for it and see what happens. If not, aim for consistency.*

2. Engage with others.

Whether that be posts, messages, comments and requests, engage with all of these aspects of LinkedIn. By engaging with other people's posts, by writing a thoughtful comment, your voice will be added to the conversation and show up where you want it to be. Look at the posts of your ideal clients and people from your target market, these are the posts you want to be engaging with. It also endears you to others, and allows you to start building trust. When people comment on your posts, how do you feel about them? I've found that it makes me want to engage with them further and, potentially in the long run, do business with them. When people do engage with you, ensure that you engage back otherwise it appears that you don't respect their opinions or you're not bothered about what they have to say. Something that works well is checking the likes on your posts, are you in contact with these people? If not, reach out to them. They have taken the time to engage with you, so you should do it back.

3. Build your pipeline and network.

Do this by accepting connection requests, checking out employees from companies within your pipeline, and sending requests to those who engage on your posts, or on posts you have commented on. If you aim for 20 per day (which can take minutes), you will grow your network by 140 each week or 7,300 per year. In no time at all, you will have a very powerful network. If you meet people face to face, at networking events, conferences, or exhibitions, be sure to send them a LinkedIn request straight away. It not only helps you keep and grow your network, but it shows them that you value their opinion and business

4. Try LinkedIn Events.

This is where you can promote an event you are running, either offline or online (LinkedIn Live). It allows you to reach a huge audience for your event and make it considerably more successful. Once the event is created, you can also invite all your connections to join or attend. Through offering events, your profile will be raised and you'll become the go-to person for knowledge on that particular topic. And, you never know, you may just get asked to talk and present off the back of it.

5. Be genuine and helpful.

This is a key aspect of building your personal brand, as you already know, but it can also help you to get more out of LinkedIn. Something I try to do is post about other companies. Maybe I have worked with somebody who has done a great job, and in that case, I want to refer others to them, and the best way to do that is through LinkedIn as the audience is so far-reaching. I normally post a photograph showing their work and tag them in it. I then build a narrative around it. By doing this, you improve your relationship with the person and they're more likely to want to work with you in the future. A win-win.

TOP TIP: *Take a look at other posts. If somebody is asking for help in something in my field, then I will always help them. If that person happens to be the ideal customer, you solve a problem for them and you are likely to get more enquiries and future business.*

6. Imagery, videos and podcasts.

You want your posts to be eye-catching. Social media is becoming about so much more than the written word, and has moved towards more visual information. Images are a MUST on every post. This will make them stand out. If you want to make it stand out even more, post a video or podcast. I started focusing on this just over a year ago and the interaction with my posts doubled overnight. Keep the video or soundbite snappy – 30 seconds max. You can always direct them to your website to access the full content but on LinkedIn short, sharp content gets the most attention. You want to encourage people to stop scrolling and see your content, and videos and soundbites are an ideal way to do that.

7. Empower your employees.

One thing that works wonders, is allowing your employees to post there too. You can set some guidelines, but the best ones are the spontaneous, personal and genuine ones. If you have a team of twelve, for example, and they all post on LinkedIn, imagine the traction this would get for your company. They say that the best people to write about a company are the staff, and in my experience, this is completely true.

8. Network on posts – tags and hashtags.

This is similar to being helpful, but there's a little more to it. When I do post, I always tag people, companies and trade associations it applies to. If I met somebody that day at an exhibition, for example, I'd copy them into it too. I then go a step further and tag in all the trade associations and groups that we as a company, and myself personally, are a member of. By doing this, your post has a much further reach. Most people will see it and share it, so suddenly your post goes from being seen by only your followers, to being seen by everyone else's followers. Hashtags are also key here. A hashtag is a word or phrase that people follow. Therefore, if you put a popular hashtag in your post, it will be seen by people who follow that hashtag.

An Example:
I regularly use the #ukmanufacturing hashtag as it has a large following that I want myself, and my company, to be associated with.

9. Be positive.

This is an absolute must. Don't be mean or negative or rude. People who turn to LinkedIn want to find information, learn and develop by seeing the success of others. They will likely want to emulate successful people in their fields, such as yourself, and the more information they get from your posts, the more likely they are to interact with you outside of LinkedIn.

10. Just give it a try.

You have read the best ways to set up your profile, the only thing left for you to do is to give it a go. You've got all the information you need to put your best foot forward. If you're already using LinkedIn, I hope that you've picked up some tips that you're going to implement.

Words of Wisdom from People Wiser than Me!

Here we are, the portion of the chapter where we learn from people far wiser than me. I hope that these quotes stir you into action, if my words didn't quite manage to.

'LinkedIn is no longer your digital resume. It's your reputation.'
Jill Rowley

'If you look really closely, most overnight successes took a long time.'
Steve Jobs

'Active participation on LinkedIn is the best way to say, 'Look at me!'
without saying 'Look at me!'
Bobby Darnell

Summary

LinkedIn is a business and employment-focused social media platform that has the power to transform your business. That might sound dramatic, but we are living in the age of social media, and LinkedIn is the social media of the business world. It is such a simple tool to utilise in order for you, and your business, to reach a wider audience. All it takes is a consistent and helpful approach, where you showcase the professional that you are, and your networking opportunities have skyrocketed. Avoiding LinkedIn is a wasted opportunity for all companies, business owners, and individuals. As a free tool that puts professionals (and potential customers) all across the globe at your fingertips, what more could you want? Also, as much as I want to write 'be consistent' in the takeaway points down below, from now on you can just assume that I want you to be consistent in whatever we're discussing, because consistency is key and it applies to each one.

Three takeaways…
1. **Hashtags and tags are your best friend.**
2. **Be helpful, genuine and engage.**
3. **Complete your profile.**

Leadership

The action of leading a group of people or an organisation.

You'll often hear the terms 'leadership' and 'management' used interchangeably. However, in reality, leadership and management are two entirely different concepts. If leadership is the action of leading a group of people, then what does this actually mean? I don't think the definition of leadership is a simple one, as it encompasses so many different things. My definition of leadership would be something along the lines of, *the ability of one person to inspire a team, an individual or a group of people to achieve their best and to work towards a common goal.* While I by no means think this definition is perfect, it covers the main principles of leadership. My experience has shown me that anybody within a company can be a leader, not just the owners or senior managers. In fact, I would argue that people in high-ranking positions within a company tend to be better managers than they are leaders, which isn't always a bad thing. Good managers are a necessity for any business, but they're not the be-all and end-all.

What to Expect...

In order to fully appreciate the impact of solid leadership within a company, we need to understand the difference between leadership and management, and when best to utilise each one, because there is a time and a place for both. In this chapter, we will cover...

- Leadership vs Management
- Reasons Why Leadership is Important
- Top 10 Tips for Leadership

Leadership vs Management

Throughout my career, I have worked in many different management positions, but until I joined Corrosion Resistant Materials, I didn't truly understand what it meant to be a leader, and how this skill set differs from being a manager. When you are in a management role within a company, you often find that you have to flip between two modes, leadership mode or management mode, depending on the task at hand. Let's take a look at the differences between the two.

Management
Management is responsible for organising, planning, controlling and meeting organisational goals. A manager is somebody who makes sure the day-to-day operations of a team, or individual, are performed as expected.

Leadership
Leadership is responsible for workforce empowerment, adaptive decision-making, social influence, inspiring and being visionary. Leadership gets the best out of their workforce and encourage, motivate and inspire.

When you're considering the difference between the two remember that managers manage the daily operations, while leaders empower and inspire. A leader is somebody who takes initiative, sets the vision and goals, invests a great deal of effort into achieving this vision/goal, and somebody who people follow from start to finish. They are part of the whole process, not just the box-ticking aspect of it.

An Example:

Over the last four years, since I joined Corrosion Resistant Materials, I have learned how to be an effective leader. When I first joined the company, I had a clear vision of where we could take it, and how to do that, but I had to make sure that I took the team with me. In order to do this, I had to inspire them to grow, to learn and, above all else, to put the hard work in. This went for the team, the shareholders, the stakeholders, and the wider community too. Being a leader is not easy, and is often lonely. I had to keep to the plan, adjust it as needed, and grow along with it. At my heart, this leadership was fuelled by growth and success, but it never stops, and the day that I am content with my leadership skills is the day the whole thing falls apart. I am always learning how to be a more effective leader. Leadership is about continual self-improvement, learning, and seeking new opportunities to better the team, company, and themselves.

Leaders…
- Set the vision for the managers to follow.
- Think of ideas for the managers to execute.
- Inspire people, while managers drive people's success.
- Look to the future while managers work in the present.
- Shape the future, while managers endorse the culture.

Why is Leadership Important?

Now that we know the difference between leadership and management, let's look further at the reasons why leadership is so important. While management ensures the daily running of the business, leadership...

1. Motivates Employees

A strong leader will motivate a team and those around them to succeed and achieve. By recognising hard work and achievement within a company, a leader will make others feel appreciated for what they do, and therefore motivate them to do more. Staff that feel valued, purposeful and respected are far more likely to feel motivated to succeed within their role and exceed expectations.

2. Sets a Good Example

Leaders set the example of 'good behaviour'. A true leader gets the best out of others by modelling a good example for others to follow. The more leaders you have in a business, the stronger, more motivated workforce you will have. By setting expectations high and demonstrating what it means to exhibit these expectations, staff will have role models to learn from within the workplace.

3. Creates a Strong Vision and Direction

Every business needs to know where they are and where they're going in the short term, but there also needs to be a vision/direction for the long term, so that the whole team knows what they're striving for and working towards. A leader who has a strong vision for the company, and can articulate this effectively to the team, will drive growth, as well as maintain a motivated and focused workforce.

4. Promotes Creativity

A happy, motivated and respected workforce will do more, achieve more, and bring more ideas to the table. Encouraging the creative thinking of your team can only be a good thing as they likely know their part of the business (their cog in the machine) better than you do, so their ideas may be different and more effective than your own. Part of leadership is promoting an atmosphere of respect within a company where the ideas of the team are welcomed and celebrated.

5. Improves Communication

Leadership is all about communication and good leaders will encourage this across all areas of the business. Clear and concise communication will support a company and team to function at its best, and therefore achieve more. An open workplace promotes a culture where everybody feels like their opinion is valued and heard. Communication is at the heart of everything and if a leader can improve the effectiveness of communication within a company, then everything else becomes far simpler.

In my opinion, leadership is synonymous with inspiration and empowerment, and with inspiration and empowerment, come all the benefits of effective leadership outlined above.

Top Ten Tips for Effective Leadership

As leadership isn't this tangible thing that you can accurately measure, I've found that there is a misconception that leadership skills cannot be improved; that you either have leadership potential or you don't. I don't believe that this is the case. I think that you can improve your leadership skills, just like you can improve any other skill. That being said, it's not an easy task to improve your leadership skills because there's a lot of self-reflection and improvement that goes along with it. Leadership is something very personal, so expect your journey to becoming a more effective leader to become personal too.

1. Identify your own strengths and weaknesses

To become a great leader, you first need to know where you are, who you are, and what your strengths and weaknesses are. This can be tricky because we all have biases in how we view ourselves, but it is possible. Many leadership courses start with a moment of reflection because you need to know your starting point, in order to plan for progression. One method is to ask your team to review you. Warning, this can be a very uncomfortable and humbling experience, but it is also extremely rewarding and valuable. Self-evaluation is hard, but by asking for the opinions of others, and encouraging them to be honest with you, you will learn things about yourself that you never knew. Once you have a solid understanding of who you are, you can create a plan for how to grow and improve. During this stage, it is critical that you are open and honest, if you are not, this won't work.

2. Work on your weaknesses

Once you've identified your weaknesses, you need to work on them. Depending on what they are, you could look at reading more on the topic, going on a course, or even engaging with a business coach. The important thing is that you are putting the steps in place to improve your weak areas. You can't improve all your weaknesses simultaneously and immediately, and for some of them, you may need outside support. Being collaborative in your development will support you to be successful. Remember, nobody is perfect and your team will likely feel more motivated as they watch you model self-improvement and development, which is an added bonus.

TOP TIP: *Your local chamber of commerce and local business coaches (such as Action Coach) can help point you in the right direction of resources to support your development. Often, you won't know what resources are out there until you reach out. Getting into the habit of working on your weaknesses is the best thing you will do, you won't look back.*

3. Develop a thirst for knowledge.

Hopefully, through the process of improving your areas of weakness, you'll develop a thirst for knowledge and a love of learning. If you can enjoy self-improvement, you'll find the process a lot more fun. The transition happened to me about three years ago. When I started putting in the extra effort to work on my weaknesses, I realised that I loved gaining knowledge from others, from courses, from reading, from podcasts. I just always needed to know more. I learned that it was normal to not have all the answers and that I had a lot of areas to develop (and I still do), and so I sought out the help of others who could help me to develop further. The more effort you put into self-improvement and development, the better you are able to support your team and your business.

4. Empower your team to succeed

By empowering your team, helping them to see their worth and understand what they are capable of, you will ultimately support your company to grow. Your team is at the heart of your business, people are the business, and so leaders who recognise this, and celebrate and support their teams, are ultimately more successful. Leaders must recognise their team's achievements and provide open and honest feedback, in a constructive way. This will help drive and improve the performance of the team, as well as the individual. There has to be a mutual trust between the leader and their team. As a leader, you should trust your team to perform their role, and allow them to step up and succeed. On the other hand, they should trust that you have the best interests of the team, and the company, at the core of what you're doing.

TOP TIP: *Motivated employees are happy employees. Key responsibilities need to be filtered down to the team, and the best leaders know how to delegate in a way that empowers and supports their team. As a leader, you should be* *providing your team with the tools to succeed in the tasks they've been given, whether that be through coaching or further training.*

5. Become a good listener

Listening is a skill. We might all think that we're good listeners, but if you look at it objectively, are you a good listener or are you just thinking of something to respond with? Listening is one of the most important skills a leader can have. By 'listening' I mean really considering what your team/employee says, responding to it, and actioning changes or ideas as needed. If a team member comes to you with a concern or idea, you need to be able to provide them with your full attention. This shows that you do care, and that your team members are your priority. This level of mutual respect will encourage team members to be open with you and share their ideas/concerns, which helps to keep the company running smoothly.

6. Be positive and set a good example

This can be difficult when you're having a bad day, but maintaining a positive attitude will encourage a positive attitude from others. It is important to model the behaviour you want to see from your team and, of course, you want your team to be positive. Positivity helps us to achieve more and to overcome obstacles that we face daily. By being positive, you will lower your stress levels, increase your energy and find that your confidence in handling difficulties will also improve. These changes will also be reflected in your team. If you've ever worked somewhere where the management is consistently negative, you'll know what kind of a drain this is on the rest of the team. Leaders should inspire the team, not the opposite.

7. Be decisive

Being decisive is all about confidence. By being decisive, by making decisions and following them through, you will communicate to the team that you are confident. If you're able to make key decisions, it will help the rest of your team to feel at ease, less stressed, and more willing to follow you. Making big decisions can be intimidating, but it is essential if you are to effectively execute plans and meet goals/expectations. The more you plan, stick to deadlines, seek help from others and avoid perfection, the more confident you will be in making decisions. Therefore, you'll be more confident and decisive. This shows the team that you are able to be trusted and they will follow you more readily.

8. Offer and accept feedback

Feedback is an important aspect of any workplace. As a leader, you'll be providing feedback to your team and therefore you should also encourage and accept feedback yourself. Feedback shows a person what they're doing well and where they can improve, and giving feedback to your team on a regular basis will help them to grow and develop. Feedback should always be constructive. My advice would be to always start with something positive, then move on to areas for development, before ending with another positive. A compliment sandwich. If you don't include positives at the beginning and end of the feedback, the other person is more likely to shut down and dwell on the negatives, rather than viewing the feedback as a positive experience. By being mainly positive and throwing in a few things to work on, you will build their confidence and they are therefore more likely to want to develop further and work on the advice you gave them. Feedback is all about enabling a person to succeed, and therefore should be about building confidence.

Also, it is really important in any workplace to accept feedback in return. If your team points out areas you need to work on as a leader, this can only help you grow and endear the team to you. It will show that you take on advice and listen to them. This trust and respect go a long way in creating a positive, driven workforce.

9. Set goals and communicate your plans

With any business, and especially within a sales team, we need clear and achievable goals. This shows the team the metrics of what they need to achieve in order to succeed within their role. Short-term and long-term goals help a company to grow and by sharing the plan, and communicating it effectively with the team, everybody should feel confident and empowered. When you're sharing metrics/goals with a team within your company, it is essential that you share with them how this fits into the company plan as a whole. If they don't understand the reason behind their goals, how can they possibly be motivated to achieve them? In my experience, a team that knows why they're doing what they're doing is much more effective, and this is such a simple thing to action.

10. Expand your responsibilities

It is important to understand all aspects of the business, if you are a leader, especially areas that you are not familiar with. This big-picture understanding is invaluable when it comes to planning for progression. I work in sales, and have always been in sales-focused roles. In order to be successful at Corrosion Resistant Materials, I had to learn all about the other functions in the business; accounts, production, health and safety, in order to really set my goals and align my vision with what the company truly needed.

Words of Wisdom from People Wiser than Me!

There are some incredible quotes about leadership out there from people far wiser than me, but these are the ones I find the most inspirational.

'The Greatest Leader is not necessarily the one who does the greatest things. He is the one that gets the people to do the greatest things.'
Ronald Regan

'Leaders become great, not because of their power, but because of their ability to empower others.'
John Maxwell

'Management is doing things right; leadership is doing the right things.'
Peter F Drucker

'IF your actions inspire others to dream more, do more and become more, you are a leader.'
John Quincy Adams

Summary

Leadership is the ability of one person to inspire a team, an individual or a group of people to achieve their best and to work towards a common goal. While there's a misconception that leadership is something you're either naturally good at or naturally bad at, I believe that leadership can be taught. Leadership stems from caring about what is best for your team and for your business. Leaders remember that people are at the very heart of the business and that only good things can come from empowering and inspiring them. A leader never settles, they are consistently working on their weaker areas and are like sponges, absorbing new knowledge and information from those around them. The willingness and drive to know more, to be better, and to support the team to the best of my ability is what tells me that I'm a good leader. Am I the best leader? Probably not, but the fact that I do what I can to make my team feel empowered, heard and respected, tells me that I'm on the right track.

Three takeaways...
1. **Empower and inspire.**
2. **Actively listen and take action.**
3. **Embrace the thirst for knowledge.**

Mentoring

When a person shares their knowledge, skills and experience with another person in order to help them progress.

Those who wish to learn in business, or who are new to running a business, often choose to have a mentor; somebody who has been there, done that, and got the t-shirt. Personally, I have been a mentor on many occasions, in every business I've worked in. It's an important skill to have in a leadership and management team, yes, but it is also important in life if you want to help others. I originally qualified as a teacher at university so I have always wanted to help others to progress. As my own career developed, I have been able to offer more support and impart my knowledge and experience to others who are starting on a similar journey. I have also benefitted from many amazing mentors in my career too. Everyone you see who is successful will likely have had some incredible mentors behind them in their career. Remember, everybody had to start somewhere.

What to Expect...

Mentoring is something we all have some level of interaction with throughout our lives, both personally and in our careers. I'm sure you'll remember that one teacher who inspired you, or that one boss who was supportive and encouraging. At different stages of our career, we might find that we tend to lean more into the mentor role, but there are still times when I feel like a mentee, rather than a mentor. Learning from people who are more experienced and knowledgeable than me in a certain area is something that I love, so if somebody is willing to provide some mentorship, it's not likely that I'll ever turn that down. In this chapter, we will cover…

- What Mentorship Is
- The Reasons Why You Should Be a Mentor
- Top Ten Tips on How to be a Great Mentor

What is Mentoring?

Mentoring is when a person shares their knowledge, skills and experience with another person in order to help them to progress. Maybe this is mentoring somebody inside the same organisation, or maybe it is somebody from another business. Many mentors don't even realise that they're mentoring another person – whether it just comes naturally to them, or it is a part of their job. Have you ever taught a new starter what to do? If so, you've been a mentor. It doesn't matter whether this was one-on-one or in a group setting (as many companies take on new starters in waves), if you've shown somebody else the ropes, you mentored them. Finding the right mentorship approach for you (and your company) can make all the difference when it comes to the confidence of newer or less experienced staff.

It is widely acknowledged that there are three different types of mentoring:

- **One-to-One Mentoring**

A more traditional approach, where a mentor will work with a mentee in person, one-on-one. They will be there to guide and share knowledge daily and often while doing the job at hand.

- **Distance Mentoring**

This is increasingly popular today with solopreneurs or smaller companies that do not have a lot of staff. A mentor will guide a mentee online, virtually, at regular intervals (maybe once per week). It will likely involve the mentee doing tasks set by the mentor prior to the next session – applying the learning and advice given to them.

- **Group Mentoring**

In this instance, a mentor is matched with a group of mentees. This is often popular with large organisations that hire in waves (interns and/or new starters). Some even run training weeks or adopt a training structure that they follow.

Why Should You be a Mentor?

There are so many benefits to becoming a mentor. The list that I include here is by no means exhaustive, but it will give you a good overall idea of why you should become a mentor. Being a mentor will support you to…

1. **Become a better leader.**

Being a mentor is like being a leader, but on a smaller scale. It is the perfect opportunity for you to hone your leadership skills and improve yourself, to further your own career. At the beginning of my career, I began by mentoring one or two people, and by practising and honing my skills, I was able to build on this, which led to leading larger teams and companies. Like most things, it's all about practise and mentoring is the perfect opportunity to practise your leadership skills.

2. **Improved communication skills.**

A huge part of being a mentor is being able to listen, interpret and provide clear advice. This doesn't come naturally to everybody, but it will improve with practise. Being a mentor will allow you to practise your communication skills so that when the time comes for you to lead a larger team, you'll find the transition easier.

3. Achieve personal career goals.

People often look at mentorship as something that they don't gain anything from, and that couldn't be further from the truth. Being a mentor is an invaluable experience, one which looks impressive on your CV, as it shows that you are willing to support the development of others.

4. Gain fresh ideas.

If you only ever work in one company, you will not come across new ideas often. Many larger companies are well-established and work within a set of systems that are already in place. Being a mentor will allow you to speak with like-minded business people and learn from them. Yes, you'll be imparting your own wisdom but you will also be learning in the process too. Every time I've visited a company or worked with other business people, I have taken things away that I can use back in my own company. It's all part of a continuous improvement mindset.

5. Change someone's world.

This may sound dramatic, but it's really not an exaggeration. People often seek mentors when they are struggling and they need somebody to share with them how to make progress and move forward. By being that 'go-to' person, you will help your mentee to share the load and improve themselves, and their business. This can be rewarding and addictive. Once you see the impact you can have on one person's career, simply by being a sounding board for them and offering advice, you'll never want to stop.

6. Strengthen your own knowledge.

The best way to learn something is to teach somebody else. By mentoring and training, you will reinforce your own knowledge. Many companies today have mentor programs so that everybody has the chance to train new starters. This is because it helps the mentor to revisit past learning and ultimately supports the company to advance. Speaking from experience, you may think you know something very well until you have to explain it to another person.

7. Improve productivity.

By sharing your own knowledge with others, you will support everybody to perform better in their roles. This, in turn, boosts productivity and gives you more time to complete other tasks as you can feel confident in knowing that your team can handle their roles effectively.

8. Expand your network.

Getting out and speaking to other business people, or even colleagues in your own company, is a great way to increase your network. You will, of course, meet your mentee but maybe they can also introduce you to people in their network, and vice versa. Always seek out networking opportunities and working as a mentor, or even being a mentee, is a great opportunity. People remember who helped them – so when you're mentee moves on, or moves up, they'll be more likely to help you out in the future.

9. Gain a sense of fulfilment.

This is what you usually hear when thinking about the benefits of mentoring. It is a big one, but it's not the be-all-and-end-all. However, knowing that you are supporting others can be a great personal boost and it can feel so satisfying when you see your mentees succeeding.

10. Strengthens your company.

Mentoring those around you, particularly within your own company, will increase the skillset across the whole company. Training is essential to engage, develop, and retain employees. A well-trained and happy workforce is often a loyal one. Don't keep all the knowledge to yourself, as in the long run, it will lead to you doing more and others feeling unfulfilled. It benefits both you and the staff in your company when you share knowledge and prioritise their development.

So, you can see that mentoring is beneficial both for yourself, and for the company as a whole. There's a misconception that the only person who gains anything from mentoring is the mentee, and that's not the case at all. Over the course of my career, I have benefited considerably from both being mentored and being a mentor.

Top Ten Tips on How to be a Successful Mentor

Some people are naturally great mentors, while others take a little more practise, but there's always room for improvement. Here are my top ten tips on how to be a successful mentor.

1. Set clear expectations with your mentee.

From the get-go, you need to set clear expectations with your mentee so that you know what they are looking for from you, but also so they know how much support you are able to provide. If you can only spare a few hours per week, be honest and upfront with them. Forgetting this step could lead to confusion and a strained relationship as the expectations are not being met, it could also have a negative impact on your actual day-to-day job.

2. Take a genuine interest in your mentee as a person.

From the outset, understand what makes your mentee tick. Ask them lots of questions so that you know about their business, but also about them personally. Knowing this will make it easier for you to offer the right guidance.

3. Build trust.

Trust is the cornerstone of any relationship. Your mentee needs to trust you so that they feel able to share their issues and concerns. Showing up, and being reliable and non-judgemental will help them to feel able to share with you.

4. Know when to give advice.

Don't rush into telling your mentee what to do and what not to do. You need to let them lead the conversation and ask for advice. You may well spot something that they should focus on, but focusing too much on areas where they've not asked for help won't be beneficial in the long run. It is important to listen to them, work through their concerns, and focus on the positives.

5. Share your journey.

You have a wealth of knowledge and experience so remember to use it. Give advice, but also ground it in real-life situations. Give clear examples of what worked for you and what didn't. Let your mentee know if things have challenged you in the past or if you made mistakes. As a mentee, it can feel quite daunting if your mentor comes across like they're perfect and have never made a single mistake, so share your experiences openly and honestly and maybe they'll be able to avoid some of the pitfalls you didn't. This will help you to further build trust.

6. Provide resources for your mentee.

Make sure you provide tasks for your mentee to do before your next session. You need them to make the most of the time they have away from you. You may only see them for one hour a week, but they have another 39 working hours to put your advice into action. If you give them tasks, remember to provide the resources; reading lists, web pages, podcasts, to help them complete the tasks.

7. Make sure you have the time.

Be honest with yourself, do you have the time to take on a mentee? You need to ensure that you have the time each week to be fully focused on them. It is important to be consistent and turn up when you say you will. If you have to cancel due to other things, then you need to have a good look in the mirror and ask if you really have the time.

8. Challenge the mentee.

Don't be afraid to ask questions that your mentee might not know the answer to. You have to stretch them and make them think outside the box. By challenging them to think deeply or explore things they don't know, you are helping them to improve and grow.

9. Help with the little things.

Many people go into business because they are good at something fairly specific, but that doesn't necessarily mean that they are good at *business.* It may be that your mentee needs help with little things like crafting emails, creating a presentation or networking. Each mentee will be different and some may need support with things you feel are basic, but they are a challenge to the mentee as they've never had to do them before.

10. Let the mentee lead.

Empowerment is key and the more the mentee leads, the more they'll get from the relationship. You're not there to do the work for them and hold their hand. You are there for advice and to support them to grow in confidence so that they can eventually feel empowered to do things for themselves. Following their needs allows the mentee to get the most out of the mentorship.

Words of Wisdom from People Wiser than Me!

As always, here are the words of wisdom from people who we can all stand to learn a thing or two from.

'A mentor empowers a person to see a possible future, and believe it can be obtained.'
Shawn Hitchcock

'If you cannot see where you are going, ask someone who has been there before'.
J Loren Norris

'The delicate balance of mentoring someone is not creating them in your own image, but giving them the opportunity to create themselves.'
Steven Spielberg

'Mentoring is a brain to pick, an ear to listen, and a push in the right direction.'

John C Crosby

Summary

Mentorship is when a person shares their knowledge, skills and experience with another person in order to help them progress. It does not have to be a huge laborious undertaking. In fact, it might simply be a part of your daily role or something you spend an hour doing each week. Mentorship, to me, is all about empowering a person to be able to thrive in their role, to grow and develop, and to become confident in their decisions. No mentee is ever the same, just as no mentor is ever the same. Mentorships need to be adapted to the mentee, or they won't be effective. People come from all different backgrounds and experiences and therefore one approach to mentorship won't work for everybody. I find it works best to let the mentee lead the relationship, for them to tell me what they need from me, and plan accordingly. Watching mentees grow and succeed is one of the best feelings, and it's as simple as sharing our knowledge and experience with them and giving them a push in the right direction.

Three takeaways…

1. **Let the mentee lead.**
2. **Set expectations.**
3. **Build trust.**

In Summary...

As I promised, we've covered a lot of information in this book. Hopefully, you've come out of the other side with plenty of points to put into action. Growing your business doesn't have to be complicated, and learning from those with years of industry experience can help you avoid making preventable mistakes. You don't have to do everything all at once. Perhaps it might be a good exercise for you to write down a few priorities that you're going to focus on and go from there. Nobody is expecting miracles and your business won't change overnight. Slow and steady wins the race, and consistency is EVERYTHING. I cannot begin to overstate the importance of consistency. Take your time and be consistent, do what is manageable for you and stick with it. Life is a marathon, not a sprint. So, as you go forward with your new knowledge, there are three key points that I want you to remember...

1. **You have to be consistent.**
   Without consistency, you will certainly fail. Doing something once will not enable you to see the changes you're looking for. No matter what you're doing, aim for long-term consistency.

2. **Failing to plan, is planning to fail.**
   Be systematic and have a plan. You can never over-prepare, but you can under-prepare. Not only will you feel more confident going into new situations if you've taken the time to prepare, but the outcome will likely be far more desirable.

3. **Be genuine, supportive, and helpful.**
   People buy from people. If you're in a position to be able to help and support others, they will remember that. It's all part of forming good relationships and a quality network of people. It's not difficult to be kind and genuine, and it can make all the difference.

Printed in Great Britain
by Amazon

22573770R00084